Whole Health

for happy dogs

A NATURAL HEALTH HANDBOOK
FOR DOGS AND THEIR OWNERS

Jill Elliot, D.V.M. • Kim Bloomer
PHOTOGRAPHY BY NICK RIDLEY

CRESTLINE

This edition published in 2010 by CRESTLINE
A division of BOOK SALES, INC.
276 Fifth Avenue Suite 206
New York, New York 10001
USA

First published in the United States of America by
Quarry Books, a member of
Quayside Publishing Group
33 Commercial Street
Gloucester, Massachusetts 01930-5089
Telephone: (978) 282-9590
Fax: (978) 283-2742
www.rockpub.com

Library of Congress Cataloging-in-Publication Data
Bloomer, Kim.
  Whole health for happy dogs : a natural health handbook for dogs and their owners /
Kim Bloomer and Jill Elliot.
        p.   cm.
    1. Dogs—Health. 2. Dogs—Diseases. 3. Holistic veterinary medicine. I. Elliot, Jill. II.
  Title.
  SF991.B56 2006
  636.7'089—dc22   2005032903
                                                                                    CIP

ISBN-13: 978-0-7858-2621-7
ISBN-10: 0-7858-2621-1

Design: James Casey Dzn
Production: *tabula rasa*
Illustrations by Colleen Hanlon
Editor: Brigid Carroll
All photography by Nick Ridley/www.nickridley.com, with the exception of the following:
Jennifer Cermak, 65; Tony Scarpetta, 103, 104, 110; Courtesy of Orvis/www.orvis.com, 19; Andy Todes,
Mickalady's Pepper'd Buckshot (Pep), 20; Recipes shown in chapter seven created by Donna Twichell
Roberts, *The Good Food Cookbook for Dogs*, © 2004 by Quarry Books.

Printed in China
Reprinted in 2010

Dedication

I would like to dedicate this book to my husband, Donnie, for his continued belief, encouragement, and support of all my endeavors, and to my dog, Shadrach, who is the inspiration behind all I do.

—Kim Bloomer

I would like to dedicate this book to my mother, Jeanne, who has always set the bar very high in terms of accomplishing what she set out to do; to Bill, my heartthrob, for his outpouring of love, support, and cheering; and to my current Persian cat-in-residence, Cybal, as well as the animals that are now in heaven—Lucy, my former cat, and Lickety Split, my former Keeshond—all of whom have showed me how the miracle of homeopathy really works.

—Jill Elliot, D.V.M.

Border Collie

Contents

Gordon Setter

Cocker Spaniel

Shih Tzu

Vizsla

Introduction

Prevention: Helping Our Dogs Live Better, Healthier, Longer Lives Using Natural Alternatives

Congratulations on picking up this book. Like most people who share their lives with a dog, you want the best for your companion. You are about to embark on a journey of learning that will help to keep your dog healthy, happy, and an active member of your family for a long time to come.

Dogs are probably the most loyal, devoted, and loving of all companion animals. They live their lives showing their exuberance and enthusiasm for everything from our arrival home to a walk in the park to a rub on the belly. They are easily pleased when cared for and loved in return. In fact, it's hard to imagine our lives without the enrichment our dogs bring to us.

The longer we live with our dogs, the deeper the emotional and physical attachments we develop, similar to our relationships with other human beings. We want to do everything we humanly can to increase the years and quality of our dogs' lives, because bottom line, we love them. They're our buddies, our confidantes, our companions, our allies, our protectors, and, especially, our comedians.

With over 130 million households in the United States and just under half of all UK households owning a pet—and more than 50 percent of those homes hosting more

Weimaraner

than one dog—it's easy to see why interest in how to better care for our pets is on the rise. In fact, many of us take far better care of our pets than of ourselves.

By learning to care for our dogs before they become ill—using a natural and holistic approach—we can avoid the common disorders that are becoming more prevalent in dogs today. One of the underlying tenets of this book is to advise you on what things you can actually stop doing. Removing medications and unhealthy food and lessening your dog's vaccine load can all improve his overall health. You can also consider new alternatives and holistic resources such as acupuncture, which seem to be effective in curing all sorts of conditions, including spine and joint pain. Prevention is the key to a happy, healthy dog, and through proper management of diet, nutrition, and weight, you'll see improvements even with a middle-aged dog.

Our intention is that after reading this book you will be well versed in current holistic thinking, and will feel empowered to make educated decisions about your dog's health. There are so many resources out there for you to learn from. We will direct you to these resources as we encourage you to continue your educational journey. We simply want you and your dog to enjoy the best quality of life possible.

Some of our ideas and suggestions may seem strange to you. Some of you may already be doing many of these things. If so, you are already ahead of the game and your dog really appreciates it. If you decide not to follow our suggestions, don't feel bad about your choice. After weighing all the information, you need to choose what works for you, your lifestyle, and your dog. Only you know what's right. And we respect your choice.

Beagle

Chapter One

What Is Health?

Health is more than just lack of disease; numerous characteristics define a healthy dog. These include balanced physical and emotional states, normal energy levels, and agility. In other words, health isn't so much about what is missing or wrong, but how your dog is functioning as a whole.

Holistic Care

As holistic and natural care becomes more mainstream, people are inclined to seek the same for their dogs. Caring for the "whole dog" is the key to total health. What does that mean? It means recognizing that each part of your dog—mind, body, and spirit—works together as one unit. So, for example, if you treat only the symptoms of a disease, you are merely managing it at best—not caring for your dog as a whole.

With so much technology available at our fingertips, and all the advances in medicine, it seems that the health of our dogs should be improving as well. The fact is, our dogs are living longer, they just aren't necessarily living a better quality of life.

Viszla

Top Seven Reasons to Naturally Care for Your Dog

1. Immunity. Your dog is less likely to get sick.

2. Your dog will smell and look better.

3. A well dog is a happy, energetic dog.

4. You will save money by having to make fewer trips to the veterinarian.

5. Less yard waste—if you know what I mean.

6. Your dog will be easier to train and interact with because he feels good.

7. Longevity. You'll be able to enjoy your dog much longer in life.

Environmental toxins, household cleaners, the overuse of pharmaceuticals, and incorrect eating habits have not only affected our health but the health of our dogs. But by choosing natural feeding methods, products, and cleaners, along with engaging in exercise and mental stimulation, our dogs can live healthier, longer lives.

With a solid understanding of what makes a dog healthy, and a focus on disease prevention rather than disease management, you'll be on the road to a whole, healthy, and, most of all, happy dog.

The Whole Dog

Every single part of your dog's body works together interdependently, or holistically. If one part of your dog's body isn't working correctly, his entire body and mind are affected, not just the ailing part. By understanding how the body, mind, and spirit work synergistically, you can begin to understand how to help your dog be healthy all the time. This is a much healthier approach than simply waiting for illness to set in and attempting to treat it—often with great expense. Ben Franklin's age-old saying "An ounce of prevention is worth a pound of cure" rings true for us *and* our pets.

Unfortunately, many dog caregivers have accepted common abnormalities as "normal." To help you understand the characteristics that define health—whether in a dog you've loved for years or a puppy you are hoping to adopt—we've developed some guidelines. We admit, our standards are high, so don't be alarmed if your dog doesn't measure up to a completely healthy dog. The whole-health-care approach we take in this book can help turn around the health of even a middle-aged dog. If you are going out to purchase or adopt a new dog, this book will give you a standard by which to measure his health.

When we think of the word *health*, we're all too often thinking of a lack of health rather than a complete state of wellness. The health of your dog is not determined by the absence of disease, but rather by all the parts of his body working as they were designed to work—synergistically and in harmony together. In this state, disease does not exist.

Skin and Coat

There are many different breeds of dogs, and the list continues to grow. Different breeds have different coats because of the diverse purposes each unique breed serves. Some breeds have long, flowing coats while others have medium or short coats, and some have no fur whatsoever. Part of your decision in choosing a particular breed may be based on the type of coat the dog has. This dictates the amount of grooming needed to sustain good health in your dog. Don't forget: A good indicator of your dog's health is the look and feel of his coat.

Whichever breed you choose, your dog's coat should be clean, dry, and glossy, soft, or wiry, depending on the breed's normal coat type. The coat should be without dandruff or oiliness. Your dog will shed all year long, and even more so in the summer, but excessive hair loss isn't normal. Also, the coat should not emit a strong odor. If it does smell, something is not quite right.

Breeds with short coats typically appear to have shinier coats. It's like the human with long, straight hair versus the human with curly hair. The way the coat lies flat allows it to appear glossier. The coat should be tight (not patchy), with little (if any) flakiness, and smooth and soft to the touch. Breeds with short coats include Boston Terriers, Neapolitan Mastiffs, and Labradors (shown here).

Long coats are full bodied and thick in some breeds, such as this Afghan Hound, and thin and flowing in others. For example, a Golden Retriever has a long coat that is thick and repels water, whereas an Afghan Hound has a long, thinner, flowing coat. Both coats should be soft to the touch, not brittle.

Seasonal Shedding

The purpose of shedding is to "exchange" a winter coat for a summer coat, or a summer coat for a winter coat. The winter coat is heavier and thicker to keep your dog warm in the cold months, whereas the summer coat will naturally be thinner and tighter so as to keep your dog cool and protect her from the sun and heat. During the spring, your dog will shed out the winter coat, and this is usually the heaviest shedding season for dogs. In the fall, your dog will start to shed out his summer coat for a heavier, thicker coat. This shedding is lighter since the summer coat is thinner.

Normal shedding is typically seasonal—spring and fall. However, most domesticated dogs shed a little all year round. Part of the reason is that most dogs live inside and, therefore, "confuse" the normal shedding process a bit. Some shedding is normal all year round.

The thicker the coat, the more your dog will shed. Contrary to what people may think, short-haired dogs do shed a lot. It's just that their short fur isn't as apparent as that of dogs with long, thick coats. Wiry- and curly-haired dogs shed the least, and therefore require less maintenance.

Immunity First

Rather than use sunscreen (with all the chemicals in those products today, they could be doing more harm than good), the key is for your dog to have a healthy immune system through proper feeding and supplementation. Admittedly, some breeds are genetically predisposed to skin problems and cancer, but again, the key is a fully supported immune system.

Your dog's skin should be pink, black, or spotted, depending on its breed and markings. For example, a light-coated breed such as a Golden Retriever will have pink skin, whereas a black Labrador Retriever will have black or even gray skin, and a Dalmatian may have spotted skin.

The skin should be free of any flakiness, redness, lumps, or bumps. Typically, dogs with lighter skin are more vulnerable to sunburn and are at higher risk for skin cancer. Many people today use sunscreen on the hairless part of their light skinned dogs. However, a dog with dark skin will be less likely to experience sunburn.

Dogs do not perspire through their skin, but rather through the pads of their feet and by panting.

A curly coat is coarser than a short or long coat, but not necessarily rougher. A rough, brittle coat almost always signifies something wrong in your dog. Breeds with wiry or curly coats include the Airedale Terrier and Poodle.

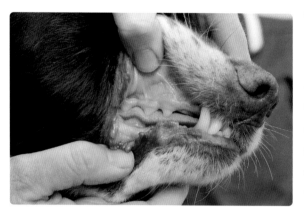

Teeth, Gums, and Mouth

Puppies have twenty-eight sharp baby teeth divided between their upper and lower jaws. By six months of age, your puppy's teeth will be pushed out and replaced by a set of forty-two adult teeth. A healthy mouth has straight adult teeth with no baby teeth remaining.

If your dog's baby teeth do not fall out naturally, his mouth may become crowded with "leftover" baby teeth, and the adult teeth will grow in crooked. If this happens, you'll want to consult your veterinarian about the best course of action to remove the extra teeth. While there isn't a lot you can do about crooked teeth in dogs, you can have extra teeth removed by your veterinarian to give your dog a more even and correct function in his jaws. Of course, with

 Chewing Machines

Dogs usually lose their baby teeth between four and five months of age. You may even see a tooth or two lying around. During this time, they will want to chew on everything. Unless you've provided the necessary dog toys and bones for her to chew on, your shoes, garden hoses, and shrubs (anything within their reach, really) may

become personal favorites of your dog. The sharp little baby teeth will eventually be replaced with full-sized, stronger, thicker adult teeth in rather short fashion.

The Breeder's Responsibility

While an underbite or overbite in your dog isn't critical or life threatening, it is nevertheless an undesirable trait in any breed. Most reputable professional breeders will eliminate a dog with this particular problem from their breeding stock. Such dogs will often be sold as pets, with spaying or neutering a mandatory inclusion in the sale contract.

pet insurance becoming more commonplace for pets and their medical procedures, such as cornea replacement, becoming a reality, braces may be next.

Bulldog

In addition to being straight, your dog's teeth should also be white. Many dogs have what we think of as "dog breath" and dark or dirty-looking teeth with a lot of plaque on them. This is not a healthy dog mouth and can adversely affect the overall health of your dog. Smelly dog breath can often be attributed to the plaque on your dog's teeth. By following proper feeding and nutrition, you can keep your dog's teeth clean and white.

In general, your dog's gums and tongue should be light pink. In some unique breeds, such as the Chow Chow, the tongue is black. In the case of a Dalmatian, the tongue can even be spotted (like the dog's coat). Anything to the contrary is a sign of something wrong. Believe it or not, dogs can have periodontal disease, so healthy gums are just as important to your dog's well-being as healthy teeth are.

Your dog's jaw should align with the upper jaw over the lower jaw. Many dogs have a "bad bite" where the lower jaw protrudes over the upper jaw. An underbite or an overbite can lead to eating problems for your dog, since the jaw isn't properly aligned. Many people find this trait cute and while that may be so, it is still not a good trait to breed into any dog. It may be accepted in certain breeds, but it really isn't good for your dog's overall health.

Ears

Whether your dog has erect ears or floppy ears, the ear canals (deep inside the ears) should be pink and clean of any discharge or odor. There might be a small amount of wax—especially if your dog likes to lie in or roll around in dirt—but it should not be excessive.

Dogs with floppy ears tend to get more ear infections than dogs with erect ears because their ear canals don't get to breathe as much. Dogs that frequently get water in their ear canals may experience more chronic ear disease. To regulate the health of your dog's ears, it is very important to establish a regular schedule of cleaning them, especially after your dog has gone swimming or had a bath.

If your dog is shaking his head a lot, scratching at his ears or forehead, or rubbing his ears or head on you or your furniture, check his ears to see if there is any sign of disease (redness, discharge, offensive odor, growths, mites, or ticks). If so, you may want to take him to your veterinarian for a checkup. When a dog rubs his head, it may be only a headache (yes, our dogs do get headaches just like we do), but it is always better to err on the side of caution when you are uncertain of what is wrong.

 Ear Cleaner Recipe

1 part white vinegar

2 parts water

Some recipes call for the addition of alcohol, which may or may not be irritating. Dogs with sore ears from allergies or infections will probably experience stinging from the solution. Ask your veterinarian to show you how to clean your dog's ears at home.

Eyes

That bright-eyed look in your dog is more than just happiness—it is a real indicator of healthy eyes. Your dog should be focused on you or whatever he is looking at. He should not have any excessive tear production or any mucus or colored discharge coming from his eyes.

Many small white dogs such as poodles or Bedlington terriers may have a continuous watery discharge from their eyes. This is another instance where people have accepted it as normal, but it is not. Such conditions indicate that something could be wrong.

You may also see the third eyelid in some breeds such as Mastiffs or Shar-Peis. This membrane protects and washes their eyes. However, if this third eyelid, or conjunctive tissue, becomes swollen or enlarged, it can irritate your dog's eye to the point of ulceration. If this occurs, you can start treatment at home with an eye wash, but it will require a veterinarian to assess whether further treatment is necessary.

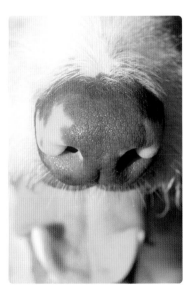

Nose

A healthy dog's nose is usually moist and clean. We've all heard that a dry nose on a dog means she is sick, but that is not necessarily so. There should be no discharge except for a clear one. If her nose is cracked, changes color, gets erosions, or emits discharge, you may want to take your dog to the veterinarian to have her checked out. Correcting this problem may be as simple as changing the type of food or water bowl you use.

Muscles, Bones, and Gait

Dogs walk on all four paws, unlike humans, who have only two points of contact (feet). A dog's weight is evenly divided between its front and rear legs. Your dog's muscles should be well formed and its gait should be even, without limping or holding any feet up in the air as he walks or runs. A well-formed muscle will be striated along your dog's flanks (or sides), the shoulders will bulge out slightly, and the hind legs will have clearly formed muscles showing their strength. Your dog's ribs should be visible but not protruding.

All dogs are not created equal, except in friendship. This is evident with a German Shepherd and his pal, a crossbreed.

If your dog doesn't look this way, it could be from lack of exercise, overfeeding, or even a medical or genetic problem. Seek the advice of your veterinarian if you've eliminated the overfeeding and exercise issues as the root of the problem.

When it comes to bones, some breeds are more predisposed to problems than others. For example, German Shepherds and Great Pyrenees can develop trouble with their hip bones, a condition known as hip dysplasia (see Appendix B, page 162, for more detailed information). Large or giant breeds in particular seem more susceptible to this problem, most likely due in part to the fact that they grow fast as puppies.

Major Muscles Groups

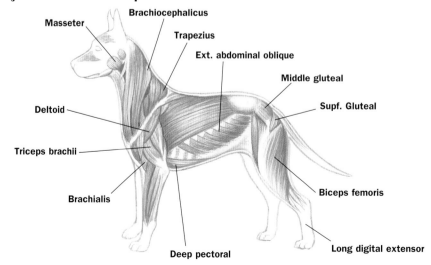

Signs of Pain

There should be no signs of pain when your dog gets up, lies down, runs, walks, or plays. If you see your dog limping, holding one leg up in the air and refusing to walk on it, getting up or lying down very slowly, or lying in odd positions to perhaps compensate for possible pain, you should take your dog to the veterinarian.

Pain can be caused by trauma (fall, sprain, strain, blow to the body, or something else), a fractured bone, a torn ligament, subluxation of the joint (bone slips out of its socket), arthritis, or spinal problems, as well as by tick-borne diseases such as Lyme disease. Lyme may cause alternating leg lameness and is often accompanied by a fever. Pain can also be caused by a foreign body (splinter, glass, etc.) in your dog's pads, a cut, a broken nail, or a growth on or between his pads. Severe inflammation between the toes will also cause pain.

Breeds with elongated backs will often develop spinal problems as they age. This may come from being overweight, from undue strain on the back muscles and spine, or from being overly active and prone to accidents. Dachshunds, Corgis, and other dogs with elongated backs are especially vulnerable to spinal problems due to their body structure. Because they have longer backs, their weight is distributed over a greater area, and their unusually short legs are spread farther apart. This can cause them to twist or injure their backs more often than a dog with a shorter back and spine might.

If you have a dog with an elongated back, the best thing you can do to prevent spinal problems is

A ramp, such as the one shown in this picture, can greatly ease stress in your dog's joints by stopping him from doing any jumping that could cause injury. It is a wise purchase for an older dog with arthritis, or one that simply has difficulty moving around.

to keep your dog slightly underweight or at normal weight for its breed. Try to discourage your dog from jumping up and down on high objects (not an easy task, as most love to jump). You may want to construct a ramp or staircase so your dog can get on and off your bed and couch without having to jump. These special ramps can also be purchased from pet catalogs and pet stores.

Weight

Dogs are healthiest when they are at a normal weight. The best way to judge this is by running your hands over your dog's body. You should be able to feel a thin layer of fat between the rib cage and the outside of the dog's body, and you should feel an indentation (a waist) behind the rib cage as you move your hands backward on the dog's body. When you run your hand down your dog's back, you should feel a nice flat back, not a protruding spine or hips.

If the ribs and spine are prominent, the dog is too thin. If there is a lot of fat between the ribs and the outside of the body or there is no waist, your dog may be overweight. Being overweight is especially dangerous in dogs with elongated body types because of the extra strain it places on their back. Being overweight is one of the most common causes of all back and joint problems. It can also predispose your dog to other

Manchester Terrier

Left: With an overweight dog, you will not easily feel her hips or ribs, but you will still be able to feel her spine through her skin. When viewed from the side, her stomach will not tuck up into her ribs at all, and from above, her sides will appear widened, with almost a barrel-type shape. Obese dogs possess these same characteristics, only they are more exaggerated: you can't feel her spine through the skin, her belly hangs down, and she is very wide when viewed from above (with absolutely no waist whatsoever).

Below: If your dog is emaciated, her ribs, spine, and hip bones will be easily felt and seen because she won't have any fat between the bones and her skin. When viewed from the side, her stomach will tuck way up into her body, and when viewed from the top, she will have a severe hourglass shape. An underweight dog will have similar attributes, though not as severe.

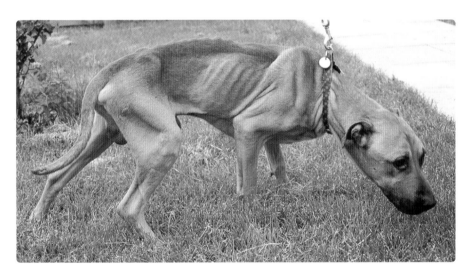

health problems such as diabetes. So, achieving the ideal weight is not only great for your dog's overall health, but it will prevent common diseases from occurring even if your dog may be predisposed to them.

The dog of ideal weight has a decent amount of fat between her skin and her ribs, hips, and spine, and you can actually feel the bones. When viewed from the side, her stomach is tucked in, with good muscle coverage. From above, her waist is evident, and again, her muscle is visible.

Energy

Most young dogs have boundless energy. It is not uncommon for puppies and some older dogs to play for hours with their toys, or to run and play in the park or yard, especially if they are with some of their dog buddies. But as they age, their energy levels may decrease.

Your dog's breed will largely determine his activity level. Some breeds are much more energetic than

German Shepherd

others. For example, a Jack Russell terrier is highly energetic (all terriers are, for that matter) and may be described as practically bouncing off the walls. My friend's terrier is notorious for bringing his ball to her so she will toss and he can fetch—which he can do for hours on end. He is still doing this at age seventeen. A Basset Hound, however, will be very happy to lie around "relaxing" until there's a call to the food bowl. There is great variation in normal energy levels among the different breeds.

Read up on different breeds to find a dog that matches your energy level before you bring it home. Otherwise, you may have a conflict of personalities to deal with for many years to come.

Your dog's energy level also may be determined by what she eats. If you are feeding your dog something that her body can't fully assimilate and utilize, her energy levels will be lower than what would be considered normal for her breed. (See chapter seven for complete details on feeding.)

A lack of energy is often the first sign that your dog may be ill. For instance, if your dog is continually lying around and not responding to you when you call, or not getting up as frequently to eat or go out, you should take her to the veterinarian to make sure there aren't any medical problems causing this change in behavior.

Attitude and Personality

A healthy dog has an outgoing, friendly, curious, and happy personality. Some breeds may have different inbred characteristics that they will exhibit as puppies right from the beginning. The working breeds, such as Border Collies, Old English Sheepdogs, or Australian Shepherds may try herding you, the other animals in the house, or your kids. Usually they'll do this by nipping at the heels of you, your children, or other pets.

The protective breeds such as the Chow Chow, Doberman Pinscher, or Rottweiler may be overly protective and even get between family members when they disagree. The terriers seem to be more stubborn and require a lot of exercise.

When choosing a new dog, be sure to read about and thoroughly research the breed to prepare yourself for what natural characteristics to expect, and to make sure the dog's characteristics match your lifestyle.

When selecting a puppy from the litter, look for the outgoing, friendly one as opposed to the one hiding in the corner or the one fighting off all the other puppies for a toy. That puppy could be a real problem down the road, so make your observations, and choose wisely—with your head, not with your heart.

Top to bottom: Newfoundland, German Shepherd, Golden Retriever

Breeds

All dog breeds were originally developed with a specific function in mind. The Golden Retriever was derived from several other breeds for hunting near water. The Saint Bernard was used to pull carts and carry heavy loads, so he had to be very big and strong. Most terrier breeds had to be fearless, fast, tenacious, and energetic to hunt the type of animals they were designed to hunt. Other breeds, such as the German Shepherd or Mastiff, were created to protect property and livestock.

When you decide to get a dog, it is very important that you consider all the different variables. For example, if you know you won't have the time or interest to perform the necessary grooming for a long-haired dog such as a Chow Chow, then this dog just isn't for you. If you want a dog that will go running and hiking with you, adopt one with high energy that can handle such activity. By knowing and understanding the characteristics of the breed you are interested in, and by researching the needs and care for each, you will be able to make the best choice of dog for your lifestyle. See the breed chart on page 160, in Appendix A, for more detailed information on this subject.

Healthy Dog Checklist

Just like us, our dogs need to have regular checkups. Although they will give us warning signs when something isn't right, we need to be able to detect these signs before they become a problem or disease. By knowing your dog's normal ups and downs, performing regular care at home, and having annual veterinarian checkups, you can often prevent your dog from becoming ill in the first place.

Proper diet	Kibble is the least desirable form of nutrition for optimum health in your dog (see chapter seven).
Supplementation	Provide whole food-type supplements to balance out any lack in the diet, especially if you feed kibble (see chapter seven).
Normal appetite	No difficulty swallowing or chewing.
Healthy coat	Keep your dog's coat shiny and clean, with no flaking or excessive hair loss.
Proper regular grooming	Grooming includes cleaning ears, trimming nails, bathing, and brushing.
Clean teeth	Tartar build-up and smelly breath are not normal or healthy for your dog. Brushing teeth helps keep teeth and gums healthy.
Pink, moist gums	Smelly mouths and very red gums could indicate a problem. White gums mean there is a definite problem.
Clean ears	No odor, swelling, or discharge should be evident.
Comfort	Constant scratching and itching are not normal, even for a dog.
Absence of pests	Ticks, fleas, lice, and mites are not normal on a dog. Homeopathic shampoos and supplements will help.
No bumps or lumps	This is especially important if they are oozing, increasing in size, or changing color. See a veterinarian.
Healthy nose	No discharge, cracks of erosion, and moist most of the time.
Normal water consumption	Not excessive, nor minimal.
Happy eyes	Eyes should be bright, clear, and free of discharge.
Normal walking and running	No limping, favoring a leg or foot, or stiffness should be evident.
Normal bowel movements and urination	Excessive urinating or diarrhea could indicate a problem. Normal bowel movements are formed and solid, and urination should be according to water intake.

Chapter Two

What Is Disease?

Once a dog is diagnosed with a disease, the questions most commonly asked by the caregiver is, "Why did this happen?" and "Was there something I could have done to prevent this," or "Did I do something wrong?"

Humans often look to their heredity for answers as to why they come down with different illnesses. But in the animal world, we rarely know the health history of our dogs' ancestors. This makes it very difficult for the dog's caregiver to accept that a disease may have developed just because of genetics or the "luck of the draw." Just as difficult to accept is the occurrence of acquired diseases, which are not controlled by genes.

Congenital Disease

Some genetic defects can affect all breeds, while others tend to be breed-specific. Once a genetic defect is discovered in a line, a good breeder will stop using the dogs that produced that trait in order to breed out the defects. For instance, if the breeder notices that some male puppies' testicles do not descend, he should stop using whichever male dog was used to sire those puppies, and neuter him. Serious illness can occur if an undescended testicle(s) is not removed, and the new caregiver faces the added expense of a surgery requiring an incision into the dog's abdomen. An ethical breeder should take considerations such as these into account when selling a puppy, and strongly recommend neutering him so that he is unable to pass on this genetic trait.

 Inbreeding

Inbreeding occurs when dogs of the same line are bred with one another. For example, the breeder may decide to breed the male offspring back to the mother, or the siblings of a same litter together. This does not allow for a good mix of genes and may cause a recessive trait to come out more prominently in a line of dogs. Congenital diseases specific to a breed, such as heart disease in Cavalier King Charles Spaniels or hip dysplasia in German Shepherds, will be more prevalent in the offspring of inbred animals. However, this may show up in a regular breeding mixture as well.

Breed-Specific Diseases

Some genetic abnormalities apply to the small dogs, such as Shih Tzu, which often develop protruding lower jaws. Although not life threatening, this is an undesirable trait that can cause crowding of the teeth. This misalignment of the jaw can lead to problems for the dog when eating, and cause added buildup of tartar between crowded teeth. This in turn might require the dog to have more than the average amount of dental cleanings.

Another example of a breed-specific disease is the presence of cataracts in Poodles. These are often present at birth but may not be visible until two months of age, and may develop anytime up to six years of age. This can cause blindness in some dogs that are affected at a very young age. However, the cataracts may also spontaneously disappear. Parents of these dogs as well as previous litters of these parents should be screened by the breeder before selling the puppies.

Hip Dysplasia in Large Breeds

Hip dysplasia may be caused by genetics or acquired with old age. The genetic form is the worst kind to have, as puppies are extremely active and the disease will greatly affect their mobility. It happens when the ball and socket of the hip joint do not fit perfectly as they were meant to fit. The head of the femur (thigh bone) may be flattened rather than smooth and rounded, or may not fit securely into the hip socket (pelvic bone). The ligaments may be lax, and have less joint fluid. All of this causes instability and pain as the dog moves around.

With hip dysplasia, your dog's rear end often sways and sometimes slumps. For a large dog, this causes problems with mobility, especially going up and down stairs and getting into and out of the car. Take your dog in for an X-ray if you see signs of pain in the rear quarters. By the time the dog is two years of age, you should know whether he has the genetic form of hip dysplasia.

This problem can often be controlled with nonsteroidal painkillers (from your veterinarian), as well as with supplements, massage, chiropractic treatment, homeopathy, or acupuncture. (See chapter four on alternative treatment modalities.)

Hip and elbow dysplasia is a disease Rottweilers often face. This is due in part to their large size and also to improper nutrition or feeding of commercial pet foods, which do not supply all the nutrients needed for large-breed dogs who grow rapidly.

If the pain becomes too severe, the dog might need a hip replacement surgery on one or both hips. This can be very costly. If you are going to have this surgery performed, please find a board-certified orthopedic surgeon. Your dog can have only one hip replacement at a time, which gives you the opportunity to evaluate how much better the dog is after the first surgery before even considering doing a second surgery. Many large dogs with severe problems of this sort are sometimes given away or euthanized because their owners cannot manage their condition.

For more information on breed-specific diseases, see Appendix B, which lists common congenital problems in certain breeds.

Acquired Common Diseases

Many diseases may affect your dog over his lifetime, regardless of his genetic history. Some of these include cancer, arthritis, allergies, and spinal disease. But if you follow the suggestions we present throughout this book, you may be able to prevent your dog from acquiring these diseases.

Cancer

Cancer is a very large topic all by itself. Unfortunately many dogs succumb to different forms of cancer. There are many reasons for this. Sometimes we might be able to discover genetic, environmental, or vaccine-related causes. Oftentimes, however, no specific reason can be determined.

Female-Specific Cancers

There are a few cancers you, as a responsible dog caregiver, can help to prevent.

Breast cancer in female dogs can be prevented by spaying your dog before the fourth estrus (period) or before the age of two and a half years old. The reason for this is most likely due to the fact that 50 percent of dog breast cancers are estrogen related. If the dog is spayed young, then estrogen won't be a problem when the dog gets older (breast cancer usually develops after about age six).

Spaying the female dog when she is young also prevents another disease, called pyometra (an infected uterus). This usually occurs in unspayed female dogs over the age of seven years old, and again is due to the estrus cycles. However, I have personally seen this condition occur in a two-year-old female dog.

Pyometra is a very serious condition and the only treatment for it is surgery in the form of a hysterectomy. Anytime a sick dog is taken into surgery, the immune system is further depleted, increasing the risks of the surgery itself. Needless to say, your dog is a much better candidate for this surgery when she is six months old—the recommended time to spay a female dog.

Male-Specific Cancers

Male dogs with undescended testicles are prone to develop testicular cancer. (The testicles should never be kept internally, where the temperature is warmer than normal.) Therefore, it is recommended that all dogs with undescended testicles be neutered. This will accomplish two important things: preventing future cancer from developing and preventing these dogs from breeding and passing on this problem to their male offspring.

More common for larger breed male dogs that are not neutered is cancer of the anal sacs in the rectal area. This is also treated with surgery to remove the cancerous growth, in addition to neutering the dog to remove the cause of the cancer. These tumors are hormone-related and are seen in older, intact male dogs.

Arthritis

Another common disease is arthritis. It is usually seen in older dogs, especially large, overweight dogs. Fortunately, you can help forestall this problem by making sure your dog adheres to a healthy diet and maintains a normal weight. Less frequently, arthritis is a result of immune-mediated factors.

There are two forms of immune-mediated joint diseases in dogs: erosive and nonerosive. Although this is not a common disease in dogs, it can cause lameness. The erosive form is similar to rheumatoid arthritis in humans and is more common in toy- and small-breed dogs. It can strike at four years of age or older, destroying the connective tissue. Signs are swelling of the joints and lameness that may alternate between different legs. These are also signs of Lyme disease, so it is important that a blood test be done to differentiate the two diseases.

The nonerosive form of arthritis is more common in medium-size and large-breed dogs. Usually this strikes at five years of age or older. Dogs may appear lethargic, have swollen joints, and look like they are "walking on eggshells." It is caused by deposition of immune complexes in the synovial tissue (the soft tissues surrounding or lining the joints), which causes inflammation. This form of arthritis is called systemic lupus erythematosus. In lay terms, this is an autoimmune response to a normal bodily function. The body is attacking itself and the cause is unknown.

We highly recommend working with holistic veterinarians to treat arthritic conditions. Holistic treatments often work very well when a dog does not respond to conventional medicine.

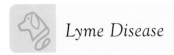

Lyme Disease

Lyme disease is a very common acquired disease, especially in dogs that live or spend spring, summer, and/or fall in wooded areas where lots of deer are present. Hunting dogs have the highest probability of being exposed to this disease. It is most commonly passed to dogs by the bite of an infected deer tick (*Ixodes dammini*). However, other insects such as horse flies can also carry and pass on Lyme disease to dogs and people.

Lyme disease primarily affects the joints. You may notice your dog limping on his left leg one week and his right leg the next week. The joints may

Four Stages of the Deer Tick

It is important to be able to distinguish between a deer tick and a wood tick. The deer tick, *Ioxdes scapularis*, is the one that actually carries Lyme disease. Wood ticks are more of a nuisance than a carrier of disease. Here, you can see the various life stages of a deer tick. It is extremely small and very hard to detect. Only when it reaches adulthood does it become close in size to the average wood tick. Being able to distinguish between the two types of ticks is very important when checking your dog (or yourself). If a deer tick appears to have been on your dog for some time, and Lyme disease is common in your area, it is best to have him tested for the disease—especially if he is showing symptoms..

become swollen and the dog may have a fever. Together, these signs all point to Lyme disease, and you should bring your dog in to the veterinarian to get checked out.

A veterinarian will administer a blood test to determine if your dog has Lyme disease. If the dog has been vaccinated for it, he will always test positive to the first screening test. Therefore, a second test, called the Western blot, will be necessary to determine if the positive reaction is from the vaccine or from exposure to the disease. Whether or not your dog is showing clinical symptoms, if the blood test is positive for Lyme Disease, most conventional veterinarians recommend treating the dog with antibiotics for fourteen to twenty-one days. Dogs with active signs of the disease will show a quick response to the medicine and symptoms will be alleviated. Often, the antibiotic will resolve the problem completely, but if not, a different antibiotic will be administered and a longer course of treatment may be necessary.

To prevent Lyme disease, limit your dog's access to tick-infested areas. Make sure you apply an all natural essential oil tick repellent as outlined in chapter nine whenever you know your dog may be in a tick-infested area. Check your dog for ticks every time he or she comes into the house. Look between the toes, in the ears, in the nose, on the belly, and in all the groin areas. If you have a dark and thick-coated dog, ticks will be very difficult to locate. You must be vigilant in checking the whole dog and using good tick repellent.

Many people ask me if chemical tick repellents are good for their dog. Although I prefer to use as few of these products as possible, I always recommend them when the lifestyle of the dog dictates their use. Of course, you can also consider the Lyme vaccine if you know your dog will regularly face heavy exposure to ticks. However, this is one vaccine that does not have a lot of information on its effectiveness, and it may not be a good idea to use it on dogs already infected with Lyme disease. The best protection is to check your dog thoroughly and often and use an all natural tick repellent.

Your dog, like this Gordon Setter, can come into contact with ticks in numerous ways. Some of the most common places for ticks are in dense woods and in fields that are not regularly mowed. Generally, any place where deer live and feed is a common habitat for the most dangerous of all ticks—the deer tick.

Allergies

Allergies are a very common problem among dogs. Unfortunately, it is often difficult to determine the cause of the allergy. Usually the dog will scratch, bite, and lick at his skin or rub himself on the floor or against the furniture or walls of your home. If left untreated, your dog can do damage to his coat, face, eyes, feet, or wherever he is feeling itchy. If this continues, you will then see hair loss, a moist reddened area, scaling, and/or discolored skin (darkened area).

Sometimes the location of the lesions on your dog can point to the cause. Often flea-bite allergies will be most noticeable on the rear end of the dog, on the rump, the base of the tail, the thighs, the belly, and between your dog's legs. Dogs are allergic to the saliva of the flea. This can be so severe in some dogs that even once the fleas

This Chinese Shar Pei suffers from skin allergies.

are killed the allergic reaction remains and causes all of the above listed problems.

Oftentimes dogs are allergic to their food, particularly if they are eating kibble or commercial dog food. (See chapter seven for clarification and further discussion.) Most food allergies are expressed by itchiness on your dog's face and feet. If you suspect this to be the cause of the allergy, the first thing to do is to change your dog's food to a holistic brand (a food without by-products). If your dog is eating a dry kibble, the way to find out if it has by-products is by looking at the canned version of the same food. If the canned version does not indicate that by-products are used, then the dry version most likely does not contain by-products either. Holistic practitioners commonly find that

Whenever you change your dog's food, he may get diarrhea for a short time, so it is best to gradually add the new food to the old food over a period of a few weeks before completely switching over.

within a short time of switching a dog to a natural diet, many times a raw meat diet, the dog's allergies resolve on their own.

Dogs can also be allergic to the pesticides and herbicides you use in your yard or home. They are often sensitive to cleaning products and may develop an allergy to them. Using natural, biodegradable products is always much better for your dog (and you), even if your dog does not appear to be outwardly allergic or sensitive to these products. The effects of chemical irritants are cumulative, so eventually you will notice problems. (See chapter twelve for more on this subject.)

Like us, dogs can also be allergic to pollen and dust. Fortunately, these types of allergies can be alleviated if not eliminated altogether by boosting your dog's immune system through proper diet and nutritional support. (See chapter seven for further elaboration on this subject.)

A veterinarian will perform numerous tests to determine the cause of the symptoms. These tests include skin scraping to look for mites, a fungal culture on some of the hairs removed from the affected areas, or even a biopsy of the skin in the area to rule out other diseases or to get a diagnosis of inflammation. If you go to a veterinary dermatologist, he or she will perform allergy tests on your dog just like the ones done on people. They will shave an area on the dog's side and implant many different substances your dog may be allergic to. Then they will read the results to see which of the spots show a reaction to the material implanted in that area. Once these allergenic substances are determined, the dermatologist may suggest giving your dog allergy shots, just like the ones given to humans.

Treatment of dogs with allergies can be very frustrating and may require the dog to be on medication his entire life. We strongly suggest you seek out a holistic veterinarian. Holistic medicine may be more effective in controlling and curing this problem because it emphasizes treatment of the whole dog. This type of treatment can potentially save you and your dog from a lifetime of antibiotics and steroids. (Steroids are the main treatment administered for this condition by most conventional veterinarians.)

This Long-haired Dachshund enjoys a loving belly rub from his owner.

Stress

Stress is unhealthy for people and pets. Many dogs seem just fine, but when faced with a major stress, they start showing signs of illness. We are not saying this to make anyone feel guilty, just to alert you to the times when you know your dog may be under added stress. These include:

- moving to a new home

- boarding in a kennel (this disrupts the dog's usual routine and isolates him from his loved ones)

- death of another pet in the household

- death or departure of one of the dog's caretakers (perhaps the person goes on vacation, a daughter or son goes off to college, the husband and wife divorce, etc.)

During all of these times, the caregiver should be alert to the possible negative effects of stress. It's a time to add extra care, love, perhaps even some supplements and vitamins to the diet, to help the dog's body and psyche deal with the added stress.

Moving On

In these first two chapters, we gave you the gold standard of health for you to try to achieve with your dog. For the potential dog care giver who is searching for a new furry friend to bring home, we hope we have provided you with guidelines and enough information to make an informed choice about your new dog.

In addition to the information we've provided about disease, please consult the chart of common health problems and suggested treatments, located in Appendix C.

Chapter Three

Health-Care Considerations: Choosing the Care That Is Right for Your Dog, and the Best Person to Provide It

Even before you get a dog, start talking with other dog owners in your neighborhood and ask them which veterinarian they use. Most likely, you will learn of three to five veterinary offices with good recommendations. We suggest that you contact each office and then choose the one that provides the best options for you with respect to hours, availability of veterinarians, emergency services, fees, and whatever else is most important to you.

When you call each veterinary practice, explain that you are getting a new dog and would like to know what usually happens on the first visit, and what vaccine protocols

Yorkshire Terrier

Questions to Ask Other Pet Caregivers

What do you like or dislike about your veterinarian?

Where is the office located?

What are the office hours?

What is the cost of care at this practice for an initial visit? A regular visit?

How many veterinarians work at the practice?

Are you satisfied with the veterinarian and the service provided by other support personnel?

What do they do about emergency care after office hours?

Does this veterinary practice make house calls?

they follow. People with new dogs, especially puppies, have many questions. The veterinarian and his or her staff will want to answer all your questions thoroughly, and therefore may charge more for the initial visit. Inquire about the standard fees for different types of services so you know where you'll stand financially.

Also ask about their emergency call policies. Do they see emergencies after hours, or provide an emergency number that you can call to have a veterinarian or technician call you back? Or, do they refer all emergencies to a local (or not so local) emergency hospital? If so, is this a hospital that is open only at night and then the patient is transferred back to the local veterinarian the next day, or does the patient stay at the emergency hospital for the entire course of treatment? These are all important questions to consider when choosing a vet.

You can even request a brief visit to the office to meet with the veterinary staff, if you think it might be an important factor in making your decision. When you meet the veterinarian, look for someone with whom you feel a genuine connection. This person will be someone who will understand that you are perhaps nervous about your new dog, and will figuratively hold your hand while you express your concerns. Seek out friendly, caring, helpful support staff, including secretaries, veterinary technicians, animal handlers, and whomever you deal with at the office.

As soon as you purchase or adopt a dog, schedule a visit to your chosen veterinarian. This is so that your veterinarian can check out your dog as soon as possible in case he needs any immediate care. Also, so you can get off on the right foot right with your new furry friend.

How to Create a Lifelong Relationship with Your Vet

You want to work with a veterinarian whom you will enjoy seeing and speaking with over the many years ahead with your dog. If for any reason you are ever unhappy with the treatment or anything else at your veterinarian's office, write a letter to him or her or call to let him or her know exactly what happened and your feelings about it. If you have a veterinarian who cares about you and your dog, she will want to know if anything has happened either inadvertently or unavoidably to upset you. Most veterinarians are very committed to providing the best care and service to all their clients. Please give your veterinarian a chance to discuss any problems, just like you would with a friend or life partner.

Of course, you have to realize that a veterinary clinic can be a very busy place, and sometimes may be involved with an emergency case that demands immediate care. So occasionally you may have to wait longer than expected, or may not be able to get to speak with your veterinarian when you call. Try to take this in stride, and request to know when the veterinarian will be able to call you back so you can plan to be available at that time.

Is a Microchip for Your Dog?

A microchip is a rice-grain-size metal chip that stores an identification number unique to your dog. It gets implanted under your dog's skin behind his or her shoulder blades. This procedure is safe and usually painless, but if you have any concerns, you can request that your veterinarian do it when your dog is spayed or neutered and is under anesthesia. However, doing this while your dog is awake should not cause him any distress, nor does the chip have any bad side effects.

Once the chip is implanted, it can be scanned using a handheld device. The scanner will detect an ID number that is unique to this chip. Once it is implanted, you will be given information to register your dog and your contact information with a nationwide organization.

The benefits of implanting a microchip in your dog are numerous. We never expect anything bad to happen to our dogs, nor do we think we will ever let them out of sight or get separated from them. However, unforeseen things can and do happen. Dogs get off their leashes, jump out of cars, and run out of their homes and yards. If your dog is ever lost and brought into a shelter in the United States, the first thing the personnel will do is scan for a microchip. As soon as one is discovered, the shelter will contact the nationwide organization to get your contact information so that they can return your precious pet to you.

Veterinarians also have this scanning device, so if anyone brings them a stray, they can also look for a chip and get in touch with the dog's owner. Unfortunately, some dogs are stolen; these dogs will not be taken to a veterinarian for the purpose of finding the rightful owner. Therefore it is wise to report the loss of your dog to veterinarian offices throughout your area, so that the staff can scan all dogs of the same breed coming into their office and potentially snag a dog snatcher.

For all of the reasons mentioned above, we highly suggest you microchip your dog. It's a onetime procedure that can save you much heartache should you ever be separated from your beloved dog.

microchip placement

A Tail-Wagging Ending

Recently someone brought a stray into a hospital I work at in Manhattan. It was the cutest golden retriever mix dog, probably no more than seven months old. It had no collar or other identification on it. We scanned the dog and fortunately it had a microchip. We were able to contact the owner in the Bronx, nine miles away, who was reunited with his dog the next day. Without the microchip, he never would have found his dog.

Spay or Neuter: Being a Responsible Pet Caregiver

While spaying and neutering may be a very sensitive subject, it is also a very important topic to discuss in depth. There are numerous ethical and medical reasons why spaying or neutering your dog is one of the more important things you can do. The responsibility for your dog lies solely with you: the caregiver or guardian.

After being spayed or neutered, both females and males will be much less likely to roam. They become regular homebodies. They are also much less aggressive, and therefore less likely to get hurt in a dogfight or to bite a human. Spayed and neutered dogs are simply much easier to handle and control.

If you've never experienced a female dog going into heat, one of the main benefits of spaying her will be to avoid this excitement altogether. This is not a fun experience, unless of course you are a licensed, reputable dog breeder who not only understands what comes with breeding but is set up for the entire process.

 Shouldn't I Allow Just One Litter of Puppies?

English Setter

Many people mistakenly think that their dogs need to have at least one litter to be fully developed. That hasn't been determined by any specific studies to date. The best thing to do is to leave the breeding programs up to the professional, reputable breeders who study the genetics of their particular breed. Just because your dog is a purebred dog does not mean it qualifies as breeding stock.

Female dogs bleed when they are in heat, and attract male dogs from miles away—your house will become party central for all the male dogs in the neighborhood. She will whine and fuss to go outside, while the male dogs will be whining, howling, and fussing to come into your home.

Six months is about the normal time to spay your female and neuter your male dog. This greatly reduces, if not altogether eliminates, the female's risk of developing cancer of the mammary glands, ovaries, and/or uterus. In addition, you will eliminate the risk of testicular cancer in your male dog.

An additional benefit to spaying and neutering your dog is that you are indirectly helping your community. Many communities spend millions of dollars to rid themselves of unwanted animals. Often these are strays that rummage in garbage, soil public places, frighten children and elderly people, and more. Even though the dogs are only doing what is natural to them, they cause problems in society, and ultimately pay the price with their lives.

With over 10,000 humans being born in the United States each day, and a whopping 70,000 puppies and kittens along with those humans, it's easy to see how there will never be enough homes to accommodate every single puppy that is born. So what will happen when there are not enough homes for them? Quite frankly, euthanasia is what will happen. Every single year, four to six million animals are euthanized because shelters become overcrowded and there aren't enough homes for them. Don't contribute to this problem. Spaying and neutering our dogs is just the right thing to do.

Pet Health Insurance: Is It Necessary?

Since you're reading this book, you obviously want to know how to better care for your dog for numerous reasons, not the least being to have him around longer. Having your dog live longer usually means more veterinary care—even if you take the preventive measures of natural care—and this, of course, translates to higher expenses. So, having pet insurance may very well be a good idea.

Health insurance premiums range in price from $100 to $500 (£58 to £288) per year depending on the plan you choose. There are also monthly payment plans. Insurance premiums don't go up per month as human coverage can, but the price you pay may depend on the age of your dog. The older your dog is, the more restrictive the insurance policy becomes, and at senior age your dog may not qualify for comprehensive coverage—just like for humans. So, if you want to invest in pet insurance, the time to do it is when your puppy is still young.

Methicillin-Resistent Staphylococcus Aureus (MRSA)

MRSA is a staph bacterium that has become resistant to one of the most powerful antibiotics there is: methicillin. This bacterium is relatively harmless under normal conditions. However, if there is an open wound or even a cut and MRSA enters that wound, the result can be deadly. MRSA has a tendency to be resistant to antibiotics and continues to mutate with each antibiotic that is used against it. It particularly likes a weakened immune system to attack, which makes it an especially dangerous threat in hospitals. MRSA is spread from humans to animals and can be spread back again to humans. Primary prevention will need to come from hygiene in veterinary hospitals, where this is most often contracted in pets, and stopping the overuse of antibiotics in favor of looking to more natural treatments and preventions. For more on this deadly superbug, go to www.pets-mrsa.com.

People often are surprised when accidents or illness strike their younger dogs, but the fact is that they do tend to have more accidents. They may get hit by a car or suffer a broken leg or a bite from another dog. Emergency care can be very costly, but insurance offers peace of mind. You may find the plan will pay for itself the first time you have to use it.

Pricing will often depend on the size of your dog. A giant-breed dog is going to cost more than a toy-breed dog for obvious reasons. More medications and drugs are required for larger dogs, not to mention time in surgery. The alternative for those who do not have the money to pay for such costly treatment is to put their dogs down (euthanize). It is an extremely difficult decision to give up your beloved companion simply because the cost of treatment is too high, but unfortunately it happens to some people.

Before taking the leap to purchase insurance, shop around and do cost comparisons according to the coverage you'll receive. Many corporations now offer pet insurance as part of the benefits you receive as an employee, so be sure to check on that before purchasing it on your own.

Health care that was only a decade ago used on humans is now being performed on our pets as well. Dogs are getting pacemakers and cornea replacements—not so long ago that was just unheard of for pets. We want the best possible care for our pets, and insurance is one way to guarantee that our pets receive that care.

Some Things to Ask Before Purchasing Insurance

1. What is the turnaround time for receiving the claim?

2. What exactly is covered?

3. Is holistic care covered?

4. What are the deductibles?

5. What are the premiums?

6. Can I take my dog to any vet or only those on a list you give me?

7. What, if any, are the age restrictions?

8. Will this policy cover any existing or hereditary conditions in my dog?

9. Will the provider pay the entire claim or only part of it?

10. What is the term of the policy?

11. Are vaccination protocols determined by my veterinarian or by the insurance company? (This is very important, so make sure you find out the answer before purchasing insurance.)

12. Are annual examinations and routine care, such as vaccines, covered?

Is Pet Insurance an Option?

Pet insurance is just now starting to catch on in the United States. Of the 136 million dog and cat owners in the United States, only about 1 percent have pet insurance, while in the United Kingdom, the number is closer to 12 percent. The United Kingdom also offers over sixty different pet insurance companies, whereas in the United States there are only five such companies (Veterinary Pet Insurance, Pet Assure, PetHealth Group, Pet Protect, and the Hartville Group Pets Health Care Plan).

Many holistic veterinarians make house calls, as in days gone by. This approach helps to keep your dog calm by examining her in her own environment. Often, mobile veterinarians will perform an exam right outside the back of their car, in the dog's yard or driveway, as seen in this picture.

Conventional and Holistic Veterinarians

On the surface, both holistic and conventional veterinarians may seem incredibly similar. In order to arrive at a diagnosis for your dog, both will order the necessary array of tests and perform a physical exam. Those tests can include, but are not limited to, X-rays, blood tests, EKG, MRI, ultrasound, fecal tests, and more. Both types of vet often look into nutrition, environment, and lifestyle, to get a fuller, more complete picture of the best way to help your dog be well. However, it's the treatment or outlook that often varies between the two types of health-care professionals.

While a conventional veterinarian will use the results from the tests to determine the treatment, his approach often and most likely will include pharmaceuticals and/or surgery, depending on what is wrong with your dog. Traditional care often sees the glass "half empty" regarding chronic disease, or calls an illness in your dog "degenerative," which is more of a pessimistic outlook. The care focuses on disease management rather than finding a cure or changing the direction of the illness, which could be accomplished by getting at the cause of the problem rather than simply treating a symptom.

Although holistic veterinarians use the same types of tests and physical exams, their determined course of action can be quite varied and very different from the prescription of a conventional veterinarian. Holistic care looks more at treating the entire dog rather than just managing the symptoms of your dog's illness or disease. This means that while the diagnostic outcome of the tests and exams performed on your dog will be exactly the same as with a traditional veterinarian, the approach and outlook to treating the illness can be entirely different.

The Holistic Approach

Holistic veterinarians try to get your dog back to a normal state of health through proper nutritional support and feeding, and by using alternative modalities, including homeopathy, aromatherapy, chiropractic, and acupuncture. They do this by understanding what holistic means: each part of the body working interdependently together as a whole. Your holistic veterinarian will ask you about your dog's environment—the types of cleaners in your home, fertilizers and pesticides in your yard, what you are feeding her, if you're vaccinating every year, any medications your dog is currently on, and so on—before prescribing medication. The holistic vet often finds that changing or eliminating some of these environmental factors might actually be the cure.

As with human doctors, the best possible vet is one who blends the two approaches, and while there still appears to be resistance to this from conventional practitioners, times have changed greatly, to the advantage of dogs and their caregivers. People are being empowered not only with the knowledge to decide what type of care is best for their dogs, but also with the right to choose what course of action they want for their own dogs in regard to treatment of illness and disease.

The American Veterinary Medical Association (AVMA) has recently recognized that holistic or alternative medicine is an essential component to good veterinary medicine. All conventional veterinarians can practice alternative or holistic medicine if they've been properly trained and accredited in the modalities they choose to incorporate into their current practices. This has encouraged the blending of conventional and holistic veterinary medicine, giving people the opportunity to not only ask for more alternative ways to care for their pets, but to demand more options as well.

How Do You Choose Which Type of Veterinarian to See?

The first thing you must understand is that all veterinarians who practice homeopathy began as conventional veterinarians licensed in whatever state they practice. Many of these veterinarians may own or work in a private practice where they can practice both types of treatment at the same facility. So your first attempt at choosing a veterinarian could be to find a veterinarian who offers both services. (Consult the Resources section for more information.) When you meet the veterinarian, let him know that you chose him because of this, and that you would like his advice as to which treatment is most appropriate for the specific problem your dog is experiencing.

If you cannot find a veterinarian that practices both conventional and holistic medicine, you'll need to choose one or the other, and this will largely depend on your dog's condition. To get young puppies off to a healthy start, I think it is very important to consult with a holistic veterinarian. The holistic vet can advise you on the healthiest choices in nutrition, vaccines, and the overall way to approach your dog's health over his lifetime.

For illnesses, you may want to visit your conventional veterinarian, especially if you have a good relationship with him. Run all the necessary diagnostic tests, listen to what

English Setter

Never Give up Hope without a Second Opinion

Many distraught clients have come to me after seeing their conventional veterinarians. They were told that there was nothing more the vet could do for their dog, and to possibly consider euthanasia. Or the caregiver was told that she needed to spend a large amount of money to truly diagnose the problem, but she didn't have the money for extensive diagnostic procedures and didn't want to put her dog through such an experience. They refused to accept the vet's advice and wanted a second opinion from a holistic veterinarian.

In many of these cases, homeopathic treatment will positively affect the dog's condition, no matter how bad it seems to be at first. Depending on the disease and prognosis given, we have often seen homeopathy extend the life of the dog to far exceed that suggested by the conventional veterinarian. There are certainly many cases that cannot be helped or saved through homeopathy, but it is always worth trying this noninvasive, safe, and relatively less expensive treatment before giving up on your pet.

he offers as a treatment, and consider contacting a homeopathic veterinarian for a second opinion. Of course, if your dog is in a life-threatening situation, you should follow your conventional veterinarian's advice and do what is necessary.

However, it is important to recognize that holistic practitioners can also treat serious illnesses without conducting the diagnostic tests. Homeopathy works on the signs and symptoms of the case at hand. The homeopath does not necessarily need a confirmed diagnosis to treat a dog. The homeopath "takes the case," which includes taking into consideration all the elements the caregiver reports to him, includes the dog's emotional state. The homeopath chooses an appropriate remedy and asks the client to call frequently with feedback so that the remedy choice can be evaluated. If the remedy is not working, the homeopath will make changes as needed. Working with a homeopathic veterinarian is very empowering for most clients, because homeopathic veterinarians work in partnership with the dog's caregiver.

In My Experience
Dr. Jill Elliot

I work as both a conventional and holistic practitioner, and there are many veterinarians trained in homeopathy around the world who practice that way too. In my practice, I see the full gamut of dogs from puppies who come for their first visit to dogs who are having their first bout of illness (liver disease, urinary tract infection, inflamed ears, allergies, and the like) to dogs with serious diseases such as cancer, end-stage kidney disease, and autoimmune problems.

When I see dogs that have already seen a conventional veterinarian for a few visits, they have often been overvaccinated or filled with antibiotics or even steroids for conditions that could have been handled just as well or better by a homeopathic or natural remedy. Other times, I see dogs that are in the late stages of some debilitating disease. At that point in a consultation, I review the medical history and basic treatment given to the dog over time. Much of what I share with people about healthier nutrition and cutting down on the vaccine regimen is welcomed information. What I hear over and over is, "I wish I had known about all this ten years ago." This is why I feel so strongly that it would be best to bring your new dog for a visit to a holistic or homeopathic veterinarian right from the start.

Over the years, I have learned by experience that homeopathy can gradually restore health to a dog that seems to have reached the end of its life. Each and every time this happens, I feel like I am watching a miracle as the dog's condition turns around.

When to see a conventional veterinarian:

- checkups
- required vaccines
- surgery
- emergency care
- specialists
- when any conventional medications seem necessary

When to see a holistic veterinarian:

- puppy's first visit
- any time you want to try holistic care first
- for a second opinion, or alternative option for treatment to that suggested by a conventional vet

The most important part is choosing someone who is open to working with you, to listening to you, and who is willing to partner with you to provide the best care for your most treasured furry family member.

Homeopathic or Traditional Treatment?

One client of mine had two Shih Tzu dogs, a brother and sister. Both had been my clients for years and were generally healthy with just some minor medical problems. They were treated homeopathically for most of their lives and had been given very few antibiotics or vaccines.

One day, the owner brought them in because she noticed a swelling around the necks of both dogs. On exam I found that all the glands on the dogs' bodies were swollen, so I drew fluid from two of the glands on each dog. The most likely suspect for a diagnosis was lymphosarcoma (cancer of the lymphoid system), and sure enough, that was the result of the test. The owner was adamant that she did not want to do chemotherapy or even see an oncologist. She told me that the mother of her dogs had had lymphosarcoma, had been treated by a homeopath, and had lived four more years after receiving the diagnosis. The typical prognosis for lymphosarcoma in dogs is three months without treatment, six months if you treat with steroids only, and up to two years with chemotherapy. The caregiver had every confidence in homeopathy.

So I respected the caregiver's wishes and treated both dogs constitutionally with classical homeopathy (one remedy at a time to address all the different elements of the physical signs and the emotional picture I had of the dogs). Each dog received different remedies. Gasby, the boy dog, lived four more years before dying of heart disease (not lymphosarcoma). Brandy, his sister, is still going strong five years after her diagnosis. At this stage, she is in congestive heart failure but living a happy life. She also has a new adopted brother to keep her company in her older years.

The funny thing is that over the years I worked with them, each dog needed to see a specialist for different ailments. Once they needed to go to an ophthalmologist for an eye problem, and once they needed to see an emergency veterinarian because of severe limping. Each time, the veterinarian noticed the swollen lymph nodes and commented on them, advising the caregiver to work up the case and get it treated. And each time when the caregiver explained they were being treated homeopathically for this condition and it had been going on for years, the other veterinarian was surprised and wanted to learn more about how homeopathy could achieve that outcome.

Chapter Four

Holistic Care: From Acupuncture to Homeopathy

We have lots of choices in health care available to us today, including natural care for our dogs. In this chapter, we will discuss the different natural modalities you can incorporate into your new natural health-care regimen for your dog. We'll be discussing when to add these natural modalities into your dog's care, and also tell you about some things you can choose to do within the comfort of your own home. Whatever the case, knowing your options in caring for your dog will empower you with the knowledge to make informed decisions.

Malamute

Acupuncture

Do you get a bit apprehensive just thinking about the needle part of acupuncture? Well fear not, because this is one of the oldest forms of natural healing, and when done correctly, it's painless. Acupuncture is used as a way to restore balance within the body. It aids circulation; triggers the release of endorphins, which are the body's natural pain reliever; and increases blood flow to the area needing help, thus speeding up the healing process.

Chinese practitioners have used acupuncture on humans and animals for thousands of years. The exact "how it works" of acupuncture is uncertain. The theory is that an energy force, called *qi* (pronounced *chi*) by the ancient practitioners of acupuncture, flows up and down the body through paths or meridians. Whenever this energy flow is interrupted, illness and/or disease occurs. To release the trapped energy and set it flowing freely again, an acupuncturist inserts needles into the specific (meridian) points that correspond to the part of the body that is ailing. A dog has more than 150 acupuncture points on his body (see page 54).

If conventional treatment doesn't work for problems with the joints, arthritis, and just about any other source of pain, acupuncture may be able to heal your dog. Acupuncturists often combine the use of herbs with their practice to bring a whole treatment to the patient. Dogs can respond very well to this form of natural therapy. When an acupuncture needle is inserted into your dog—which is usually done very quickly so as to keep your dog as calm as possible—the muscle where it is inserted actually grabs hold of the needle and then releases it as energy is restored and balanced in that area. A treatment can be as short as several seconds and as long as thirty minutes, depending on the problem and its severity. Every single dog is different and treatment is incumbent upon your dog's particular problem. Each dog will have her own prescription for therapy, which may call for one or more treatments per week for several weeks.

Acupuncture stimulates your dog's immune system to work at healing itself, so no chemicals or drugs are given, and no side effects can hamper the healing progress. As your dog ages, holistic veterinarians will often recommend acupuncture as a regular part of his health regimen. (For more information, contact the American Association of Veterinary Acupuncture, www.aava.org, and the International Veterinary Acupuncture Society, www.ivas.org)

Acupuncture Points for Dogs

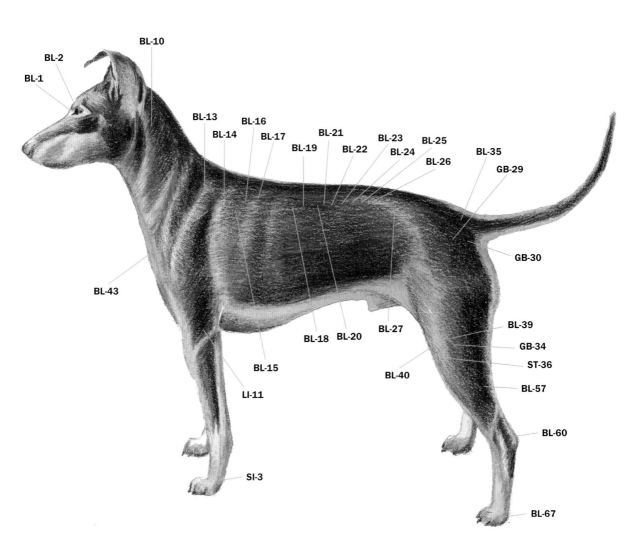

Using either pressure or acupuncture needles at these points acts to open up channels and pathways of energy, which relieves pain and restores health to the whole body.

Commonly Addressed Acupuncture Points[1]

BL-1. Jing Ming	Indications: Eye disorders: conjunctivitis, keratitis. Dangerous point because of its proximity to the eye. Avoid the eye.
BL-2. Zan-Zhu	Indications: Conjunctivitis, keratitis, frontal sinusitis.
BL-10. Tian Zhu	Indications: Cervical spondylosis, cervical disk disease.
BL-13. Fei Shu	Indications: Lung disorders such as pneumonia, bronchitis, or asthma.
BL-14. Jue Yin Shu	Indications: Cardiovascular disorders.
BL-15. Xin Shu	Indications: Heart disorders, syncope, epilepsy.
BL-16. Du Shu	Indications: Heart problems, abdominal pain.
BL-17. Ge-Shu	Indications: Chronic hemorrhage, spasm of the diaphragm, blood dyscrasias, bronchial asthma.
BL-18. Gan Shu	Indications: Liver and gallbladder problems, conjunctivitis.
BL-19. Dan Shu	Indications: Liver and gallbladder disorders. Local point for intervertebral disk disease.
BL-20. Pi Shu	Indications: Digestive disorders, pancreatic disorders, pancreatitis, vomiting, anemia. Local point for intervertebral disk disease.
BL-21. Wei Shu	Indications: Gastric disorders: vomiting, gastritis, gastric ulcers. Local point for intervertebral disk disease.

continued

[1]Schoen, Allen M. et al (eds.), *Veterinary Acupuncture: Ancient Art to Modern Medicine*, 130

BL-22. San Jiao Shu	Indications: Gastric and abdominal disorders, vomiting, endocrine disorders.
BL-23. Shen Shu	Indications: Renal disorders, urogenital disorders, back pain, vertebral spondylosis, coxofemoral arthritis, intervertebral disk disease, ear disorders.
BL-24. Qi Hai Shu	Indications: Constipation, back pain.
BL-25. Da Chang Shu	Indications: Gastrointestinal disorders: constipation, diarrhea, chronic colitis. Local point for thoracolumbar disk disease.
BL-26. Guan Yuan Shu	Indications: Intestinal disorders: constipation, diarrhea, indigestion.
BL-27. Xiao Chang Shu	Indications: Indigestion, sciatica, cauda equinitis.
BL-35. Hui Yang	Indications: Sacral coccygeal hyperpathia, paresis, or paralysis.
BL-39. Wei Yang	Indications: Thoracolumbar disease, cystitis.
BL-40. Wei Zhong	Indications: Thoracolumbar disk disease, spondylosis, caudal paresis or paralysis, enuresis. Important distal point for any lumbar or hind limb disorder.
BL-43. Gao Huang	Indications: Injury or pain of the shoulder area.
BL-57. Cheng Shan	Indications: Sciatica, pain in the pelvic limb.
BL-60. Kun Lun	Indications: Pain or paralysis of the pelvic limb, retained placenta. Local point for tarsal pain.

BL-67. Zhi Yin	Indications: To dispel wind condition, dystocia, urinary incontinence, acute emergencies, hind limb paresis or paralysis, ocular disorders.
GB-29. Ju Liao	Indications: Rheumatism of the hind limb, arthritis of the hip, paralysis of the femoral and sciatic nerves.
GB-30. Huan Tiao	Indications: Paralysis of the hindquarter, hip dysplasia, sciatica, coxofemoral arthritis.
GB-34. Yang Ling Quan	Indications: Disorders of the liver, gallbladder, and pelvic limb. Muscle and tendon disorders, myopathies, knee disorders, pelvic limb paresis or paralysis. Important point for thoracolumbar disk disease.
LI-11. Qu Chi	Indications: Pain in the elbow and forelimb, neurodermatitis, skin disorders, endocrine disorders. Homeostatic and immune-enhancing point. Often used in allergic and infectious disorders. Important tonification point.
ST-36. Zu San Li	Indications: Gastrointestinal disorders, general tonification point for any weak condition, paralysis of the pelvic limb, acupuncture analgesia. Most important distal point for abdominal disorders. Homeostatic effects in diabetes mellitus and metabolic diseases. ST-36 is one of the most effective acupuncture points, with a wide range of effects: spasmolytic and analgesic effect for the gastrointestinal tract, homeostatic effect in endocrine and metabolic diseases.
SI-3. Hou Xi	Indications: Cervical hyperpathia, shoulder pain, cervical spondylosis.

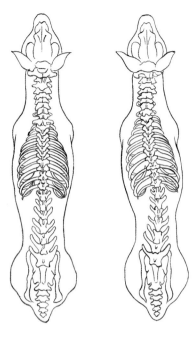

A misaligned spine not only looks bad, but it can greatly affect the overall health of a dog.

Chiropractic

Chiropractic care is based on the nervous system and function of the spine, both of which are interdependent and essential for good health. As in all holistic care, this form of natural treatment focuses on helping the body to heal itself. Chiropractic is similar to acupuncture in that the flow of energy, or circulation from the nervous system to the spine, is the key to optimal health.

The nervous system "talks" to the entire body. It is like the body's telephone system, as it is responsible for all communication throughout the body. The nervous system quickly carries information back and forth from the brain to all other body cells. The spinal column is the main control center for this communication system, and it is made up of bones called vertebrae. Each one of these vertebrae houses part of the nervous system. The spinal cord passes through the middle of each vertebra, and nerves branch out through the vertebrae and into the muscles of the body.

If the vertebrae go out of alignment, even slightly, this can affect how the nerves communicate with the body, slow down or stop the flow of energy, and throw the entire body out of balance. It's like a domino effect: If one part falters, the entire body suffers. In chiropractic language, when a vertebra becomes misaligned, the condition is called subluxation. When there is a subluxation in a vertebra or several vertebrae, nerves get pinched, stopping the communication flow between the brain and the nervous system. The chiropractor's job is to bring back the flow of communication and energy within the body by manipulating the vertebrae back into place to restore the spine's alignment. By adjusting the spine back into its proper place, the energy can again flow freely throughout the body, bringing healing from the circulatory and immune systems.

This form of natural therapy is one of the most popular for animals. One of the main reasons it is so popular is that this is a drugless form of healing, and focuses on using the natural power of the body to heal itself. Chiropractic care has a proven track record for helping dogs with a variety of problems, including those revolving around joints, muscles, and nerves. It is most commonly performed on horses, but also on dogs and cats.

Your dog will tell you when he needs a chiropractic adjustment through changes in personality (often grumpiness) and difficulty going up and down stairs or jumping. Before you start chiropractic on your dog, get him checked out by your veterinarian to rule out any other possible (especially more serious) reasons for his problems.

For more information on veterinary chiropractic care, see Resources, page 168, and the Veterinary Chiropractic website at www.animalchiropractic.org.

Homeopathy

Homeopathy for people and pets has only recently become more accepted as a health practice. This is primarily due to the public's seeking out these services, and also simply because there are more homeopaths available across the United States. Training for many homeopaths involves a four-year program as intense as medical school, which includes a two-year clinical training program.

Interestingly, before 1900, many of the world's medical doctors were homeopaths. But unfortunately, organized medical associations were established to rid the field of the competition presented by homeopathy. The drug companies, driven by economic factors, also contributed to the demise of homeopathy. Because homeopathic remedies are inexpensive and no profit could be made from them, drug companies wanted to focus on conventional drugs, where the profits would be much larger.

Homeopathy has been slower to catch on in the United States, but it is well respected and widely practiced throughout other parts of the world. It is used on all species of animals, including birds, farm animals, wild animals, zoo animals, exotic animals (pocket pets), fish, and turtles. It has even been shown effective in treating plants, flowers, and trees.

According to Dana Ullman in *Homeopathy: Medicine for the 21st Century*, a large portion of the medical professionals in England, India, France, and Brazil are homeopaths. In India alone there are over 100,000

homeopathic doctors and 120 homeopathic medical schools. Homeopathy is also practiced in Mexico, Greece, Belgium, Italy, Spain, Australia, Nigeria, South Africa, and the Soviet Union, to name only a few places. In some countries, there are hospitals specifically devoted to using homeopathy as the primary mode of treatment for patients.

The Homeopathic Approach

Homeopathy is a system of medicine that is not fundamentally used to palliate a problem; the goal is to cure. Not all cases are curable, and this may be determined by the homeopath in the first visit, or it may become apparent over time. A history of using allopathic medications, especially steroids, may interfere with the dog's ability to cure itself. Many years of vaccines and improper diet may also interfere.

Often the first thing a homeopath does is advise the pet caregiver to change his pet's diet to the healthiest food the dog will eat (see chapter seven), and to eliminate all potential obstacles to a cure (e.g., vaccines, certain medications, supplements, etc.). By doing this, the dog's condition may improve even before any homeopathic remedy is given. More importantly, it will also allow the homeopathic remedy to work better. These natural remedies are made from plant, mineral, or animal products.

A homeopath will arrange a one- to two-hour appointment with you and your pet to "take the case." This will be an in-depth interview on your dog's health history, current condition, diet, and any emotional or behavioral issues. This interview may also include questions that make no sense to you, such as those regarding your dog's temperature preferences, unusual behavioral quirks, and so on. It will be an opportunity for you to tell the homeopath all the things you have always wanted to tell your vet about your dog but didn't seem to have the reason or time to.

Homeopathic treatment is based on the whole picture of the problem your dog is experiencing, taking into account your dog's environment, behavioral qualities, and all signs of whatever illness your dog is experiencing, including his emotional reaction to it. Homeopaths that work with people rely heavily on emotions and beliefs that the people have. These are not as easy to understand when working with dogs. But many times the dog's personality is a factor in determining which remedy the homeopath will choose. Because many signs of disease are similar to one another, they may not be that helpful to a homeopath. The homeopath looks for something unusual or peculiar about the dog or the disease. For more information, contact the Academy of Veterinary Homeopathy, www.theavh.org.

Behavioral quirks—such as this Lurcher seeking out and laying in puddles of water—may indicate a problem with your dog. Though this isn't always the case, a homeopathic veterinarian will take it into account when evaluating your dog's health.

Basic Principles of Homeopathy

1. Like cures like. The homeopath looks for a remedy that most accurately mimics the disease state (and mental picture) presented by the dog.

2. Every person or dog is a unique individual and should not necessarily receive the same treatment as another person or dog with the same problem or disease.

3. The most current symptoms of a chronic disease are the most important ones—more important than the oldest symptoms. Cure is very likely to be seen as an elimination of the newest symptoms first and the oldest symptoms last. A homeopathic cure is a slow, steady, and gentle process.

4. Herring's law states that cure proceeds from the inside to outside, from above downward, on a person, front to back on a dog, and from most vital to least vital organs. The homeopath watches to see that the chosen remedy is causing this pattern to occur.

5. Use proven remedies. Remedies and the results of their use are listed in a book called a materia medica. This is the treatment bible for most homeopaths, where they can look up remedies and decide on the best one with which to start a case.

6. A dog may experience an initial exacerbation (increase) of symptoms after taking a remedy in the first week, but this is a good reaction. This means the remedy has been effective in causing a response in the dog's body. The dog's body may be throwing off some toxins, and will then respond by moving to cure the problem. This doesn't always happen with a homeopathic remedy, but when it does, the aggravation does not usually last more than twenty-four to forty-eight hours, nor does it disable the dog in any serious way.

7. A state of chronic disease exists. This principle was articulated by the founder of homeopathy, Dr. Samuel Hahnemann. He believed that the state of chronic disease is so vast that it cannot be seen in one animal, but instead we see a bit of it in each animal. Only by looking at all the animals (or people) in a group can we get the full picture of chronic disease. This concept is important because as we start to cure a problem, we often see other symptoms pop up. These symptoms should not indicate a new disease, but be seen as signs of other parts of the chronic disease that were hidden from our view. The new symptoms can be considered as arrows pointing to the next part of the disease to be cured. This allows homeopaths to gradually and gently cure the whole disease in the dog over time.

Massage

Dogs love to receive affection, so it's no mystery as to why they both enjoy and respond well to massage. Dogs are very social and interactive creatures, so not only can massage help improve their overall health, but it allows you to form a stronger bond with your dog as well.

Massaging your dog is very much like human massage. It is the manipulation of muscle tissues, and on dogs, skin, through different techniques. From a feathering touch such as in the raindrop technique to deep muscle tissue massage as in neuromuscular therapy (usually done for injury healing), massage can be done in a variety of ways.

Massage—whether done by a professional therapist or by you—brings many benefits to your dog. It helps your dog to relax, increases his circulation, and improves the level of comfort in his body. It can enhance his range of motion and muscle tone, relieve swelling in joints, alleviate pain, reduce inflammation, and promote natural overall healing for your dog. Massage helps your dog's body heal itself by increasing the flow of energy to his muscles.

Anyone can do a general healing massage at home. Your dog will really appreciate your loving and gentle approach with this, especially at first. Most often unless they are injured, dogs prefer a soothing touch, but with more pressure than normal petting.

Give your dog a massage only when you are in a relaxed mood and can provide a comfortable environment to put him at ease. A good way to start is when your dog is

Massage is just as relaxing and healing for our dogs as it is for us. After vigorous exercise, your dog could benefit from a massage to help alleviate muscle soreness and encourage good circulation throughout his body. There are many professional dog masseuses out there, but you are capable of performing an at-home massage yourself (see page 65).

Gordon Setter

By exploring your dog's body through the healing power of touch, you'll be able to catch anything out of the ordinary and establish a deeper bond between the two of you.

already relaxed and lying down. Just start petting him and move into an easy, slow, gentle massage. Don't try to hold your dog in place if he doesn't like it. Allow your dog to learn this is an easy, fun time of bonding. Once your dog is comfortable with your stroking and gentle, light massage, you can then do it for longer periods and get into more of the actual massage techniques. By doing this prior to any professional massage, you will teach your dog that this is a nice, enjoyable time for her to relax, and when the "real" massage happens, your dog will eagerly look forward to it.

By knowing your dog, you'll be able to design a love-bonding massage that works for you and your dog in your own special way. A professional massage by a pet massage therapist will be a bit different. Because the specialist will be trained in how all the muscles work and know which technique to use, she'll understand how to work with your dog's special needs for the most effective healing. Some may even choose to perform the massage in water, which is a technique dogs really seem to like since it is a non-weight-bearing massage. You have many options to consider with massage, but one regular part of your natural dog care can include basic massage by you at home.

The Raindrop Technique

This massage technique, designed by Dr. Gary Young, is a method of applying essential oils along the spine and feet using various massage techniques and reflexology. This technique is called "raindrop" because the essential oils are dropped along the spine to simulate rain falling. The oils are applied in a specific order for their individual benefits, but also for their combined overall effect on the body. This technique was designed to bring electrical and structural alignment back to the body—like a chiropractic adjustment and massage all in one. (For a source of therapeutic essential oils, please consult the Resources section, page 168.) See www.raindroptraining.com for more information.

At-Home Massage

Weimaraner

1. Roll your dog's loose skin in sections between your fingers. A common area to start is the neck, shoulders, and ears. Be gentle and don't force your dog to stay if she doesn't want to. Talk to your dog with whatever "love language" you use and just put her at ease.

2. Continue on with a couple of your fingers pressed flat against your dog's skin, and massage the muscles gently in a circular motion. If your dog relaxes, then you can increase the pressure, but if he becomes anxious or uneasy, remain very gentle or stop altogether.

3. You might want to move on to your dog's feet, but keep in mind that dogs are very sensitive about foot massages—some will tolerate it and others won't. Start by just holding your dog's paw in your hands. (This is also a good way to get your dog comfortable with nail trims.) If he responds well to that, go ahead and start massaging the foot, gently, and then in between the pads of the foot. Never be hurried; go slow and be gentle.

4. Move from the feet up the legs and continue in the gentle but firm circular motion, stroking up the entire leg. Often dogs that enjoy this will hold up their legs to you. When you get to the hind legs, work the muscles and rub gently over the knee area. Doing this after a good exercise session with your dog will ease any soreness and keep the blood flowing through his legs, and can even help to prevent leg injuries. Be easy and don't try to grind the muscles, just remain firm but gentle. If you make this pleasurable enough, your dog may eventually get to the point that he will extend his legs out for you to massage them with no resistance whatsoever.

5. Next move to the stomach or abdominal area. Your dog will most likely roll onto her back, as this is a position of trust and submission. Remain calm and do larger circular motions with both hands, or with just a finger or two depending on the size of your dog. Again, be easy and gentle because this is a sensitive area of your dog's body.

6. Another option is to do an all-over massage using large, circular motions. You can start on one side and go from the neck down the back to the legs or vice versa. Just make sure you do both sides of his body so that he stays in balance.

7. Lastly you can do a spinal massage. You are not massaging the spine itself but the muscles on either side of the spine. Be gentle here. A nice raindrop technique using essential oils will bring great healing to your dog if she's ill. (For more on essential oils, see chapter nine).

It may seem difficult to believe, but we can communicate with our pets. Dogs listen to our body language and interpret our words through our actions. We can do the same with them. By understanding how the mind of a dog works and how to "listen" to our dogs, we can communicate with them effectively.

Animal Communication

As a veterinarian, I have occasionally found that getting the help of an animal communicator has assisted in understanding what was going on with some of my patients and my own animals. You might be skeptical and you should be skeptical. Whenever you want to consult with someone who is an animal communicator, always ask him about his credentials, training, experience, and fees. You can also ask him for references from some of his clients. Any reputable professional will be happy to share all this information with you.

With many of the alternative therapies, you have to take a leap of faith. The time this might apply the most is when considering using an animal communicator to "speak with" your pet. However, every single person I have ever referred to an animal communicator, and I've referred probably over a hundred, have thanked me and found the session with the animal communicator valuable in many ways.

First, those who have taken their pet to an animal communicator just felt they had a better understanding of their dog after the session. They may have been able to understand a specific problem better from the dog's point of view. Or they may have been able to get some medical question answered or some direction as to where to seek answers. They also may have gotten a sense of their dog's personality that they didn't know was there. And some have sought out these services as the end of their dog's life, when they were trying to make a very difficult decision and wanted to check in with their pet to get confirmation on the decision they needed to make. As far as I know, there is no negative side to trying, and it can be great fun, too.

How Does It Work?

The animal communicators with whom I have worked use telepathic communication. Have you ever experienced the disappearing cat when it's time to go to the veterinarian, or the ecstatic dog when we go for the car, even though he may be in a part of the house where he couldn't possibly have heard those keys jangling? Rae Ramsey, who resides in New York City, is a world-renowned animal communicator. She sees herself as a translator between person and animal. The animal can reveal whatever he wants to and choose to hide any information that he doesn't want to reveal. She explains it as follows:

> Communication is a natural ability all living beings, including humans, possess. It is the ability to communicate with another nonverbally. Some of the ways this happens is through an exchange of images, through a sense of knowing, through an exchange of

thoughts, feelings, and sensations. We humans have developed verbal skills so highly that we have placed almost no emphasis on this intuitive gift. We refer to it as a "hunch," a "feeling," "just knowing," or a "coincidence." But animals have not been taught that they cannot communicate telepathically, so they do it all the time as part of their natural way of interacting with others. They pick up our intuitive messages regarding them all the time."

The three different animal communicators I have used all worked by first requesting a picture of the animal, then setting up a telephone appointment. Each animal communicator scheduled either a half-hour or a one-hour session with the pet caregiver and her animal (or several animals). This work is done over the telephone, so you and your dog are in the comfort of your own home.

How that works is through telepathic communication. Pictures and images can travel through the air—that's how our computers, televisions, and radios operate. The truth is that the dog doesn't even have to be in the same room or home as the caregiver. This may sound hard to believe to most of you.

Some communicators ask you to have questions prepared in advance. Most often these questions revolve around issues of health. For example, one of my clients had a cat with an annoying habit of rubbing at its throat on the left side. None of the exams and tests revealed anything wrong with the cat. The animal communicator told us that

Sometimes no words are needed to say how you feel about someone.

Good care is a way to communicate your love to your pet.

there was a mass on the left side of the throat. We finally sedated the cat and looked deep into the throat on the left side, where we found a very flat but solid mass.

Communicators can also tell you something about your dog's emotional state. Many times behavioral problems can be shifted through this type of communication between caregiver and pet. Multipet homes can move toward more peace and acceptance. The dying process especially can be transformed into a much more positive and profound experience; the person can feel more peace and acceptance of his dog's passing. There is often much guilt and fear when a pet might be close to death. Using an animal communicator at this time has helped many people assuage their guilt and fear and make the "letting go" much easier for both.

Chapter Five

Vaccines

The topic of whether or not to vaccinate your dog is one of the most important issues in this book. We are repeatedly asked about this subject. With so much at stake, it is important to understand what vaccines really do or don't do, so you can make an informed decision about what to do for your own dog.

In our experience, many dogs are vaccinated annually for the standard doggie illnesses. Unfortunately, signs of illnesses often occur as soon as a day after vaccines were given. In many instances, a caregiver will inform their vet that the dog was vaccinated for rabies one month ago and then started to have seizures (rabies is a neurological

To vaccinate or not to vaccinate, that is the question.

disease). Or the caregiver will inform their vet that her dog was vaccinated for parvo and distemper last month and is now having diarrhea (parvo is a disease that attacks the intestines of a dog). Or the dog was vaccinated for kennel cough one month ago and now has a chronic cough (kennel cough is a respiratory disease). Some of the most upsetting reports come from dogs that were vaccinated with their first rabies vaccine at three to four months old, and one month later, for no apparent reason, became aggressive to their caregiver and other dogs (rabies also causes uncontrolled aggression).

If this happened only once in a while, we probably wouldn't notice a pattern. However, it happens so often it is difficult to ignore. Before you can understand why vaccines may be harmful to your dog's health, it is important to first be familiar with the nature of a vaccine.

Understanding Vaccines

Any vaccine—whether for humans or dogs—consists of a small amount of the actual disease it is meant to prevent. So, by administering a vaccine, you are actually inoculating your dog with a disease in order for his body to build up immunity to it.

Your dog may receive a "killed" (dead virus) vaccine or a "live" (living virus) vaccine. Many vaccines are delivered to your dog as an "all-in-one," but it's much better to have separate vaccines for each disease or illness, administered with time in between. This way, your dog's immune system isn't assaulted all at once with all these viruses and bacteria en masse. Your dog's immune system was never meant for invasion by numerous viruses and bacteria at one time.

The rabies vaccine is always administered as a separate vaccine, and it is the only one mandated by law in the United States. Many states are now going to the once-every-three-years requirement. While there is no rabies in the United Kingdom, pets traveling there from other parts of the world must have a "pet passport" showing that they have been vaccinated. It's our opinion, having no more after the first one would be the best solution, because once immunity exists, it is usually present for life.

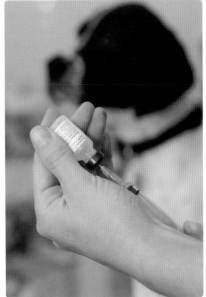

Types of Vaccines

Core vaccines (basic series of vaccines highly recommended to prevent life-threatening distemper and parvo disease in puppies and young dogs):

- canine distemper virus (CDV)
- canine parvovirus (CPV)
- canine adenovirus-2 (CAV-2)
- rabies (required by law, frequency varies)

Noncore vaccines (should be considered in special circumstances based on exposure risk):

- *Borrelia burgdorferi* (Lyme disease)
- *Bordetella bronchiseptica* (kennel cough)
- canine parainfluenza virus
- *Leptospira* spirochete (parasite)

  There are four different species of Leptospira that infect dogs. Until recently, to be fully protected, a dog must have received two different vaccines (each with two of the four species within the vaccine). There is now one vaccine that contains all four.

- distemper and measles viruses

A Strong Immune System Is Key

Typically a puppy is protected from disease, viruses, and bacteria by her mother's milk. If the mother has a strong immune system, she can effectively protect her puppies from disease until they grow stronger and build their own natural immunities. A dog with a strong immune system will be able to ward off many diseases and ill-nesses regardless of whether he is vaccinated or not.

What Causes These Diseases Anyway?

Rabies is contracted through the bite of a rabid animal. With distemper, parvo, leptospirosis, and hepatitis, contact with infected excrement is necessary to transmit the disease. In the case of kennel cough, aerosol transmission (coughing spray) is usually the cause of the disease.

When to Vaccinate

Unfortunately, many breeders and pet stores start to vaccinate their puppies as early as six weeks old, and proceed to give them vaccines every two to three weeks until they are sixteen weeks old. This is excessive and not effective. Puppies up to sixteen weeks old can still have their maternal antibodies. This is immunity passed to them by their mother. It will interfere with the vaccines being given and reduce the puppies' ability to make their own antibodies. That is why many protocols recommend giving the last vaccine after the puppy is sixteen weeks old.

We recommend that you give your puppy only two canine distemper and parvo vaccines at most. Give one at thirteen weeks and one at sixteen weeks. If your veterinarian has the new three-year distemper/parvo/hepatitis vaccine, the recommended protocol is to give it only two times—the manufacturer's recommended protocol is once at eight weeks and once at twelve weeks. However, we recommend getting your dog

These puppies are far too young for vaccines, especially because they are still receiving their mother's immunities through her milk. Vaccinating them at this point could harm their natural immunities rather than help them.

If you decide to vaccinate your puppy, three months of age is a much more appropriate age. By three months old, your puppy's immune system is more fully developed, and it is more able to handle the onslaught of vaccines.

vaccinated with the three-year vaccine when the dog is a little older—at thirteen weeks and sixteen weeks—so his immunity is stronger. Your puppy should not mix with older dogs until after the final distemper/parvo vaccine is administered.

The rabies vaccine should be given as late in the dog's life as possible. A rabies vaccine is required at about three months old. Therefore, we recommend that you follow the laws of your locale.

When Not to Vaccinate

Keep in mind it is very important to request your dog not be vaccinated if he is showing any signs of chronic or acute illness. The vaccine manufacturers state that animals with any ongoing disease should not be vaccinated until the disease has been eradicated. Unfortunately, many veterinarians continue to give vaccines annually and disregard this important statement. This is perhaps because most veterinarians have been educated to think vaccines are always good and protect the dog. Additional postgraduate education in holistic medicine provides education regarding the downside of vaccines.

The Importance of Annual Exams

Scheduling an annual exam for your dog is the most important thing you can do as his caregiver. Your veterinarian will perform a complete examination of your dog, check his stool for parasites, and check for heartworm disease. If anything isn't quite right, you'll be able to catch it and correct it before it becomes a serious problem.

Age	Recommended Vaccine Protocol
Thirteen weeks old:	One-year distemper, adenovirus, and parvo vaccine (DAP)
Fourteen weeks old:	One-year rabies vaccine (given on separate visit from other vaccines)
Sixteen weeks old:	DAP vaccine
One year later (from date of rabies vaccine):	annual exam and three-year rabies vaccine, perform blood titer test; repeat DAP if immunity is low
Second year:	annual exam, no vaccines; repeat DAP if immunity is low
Third year:	annual exam and perform blood titer test; repeat DAP if immunity is low
Fourth Year:	annual exam and three-year rabies vaccine
Fifth Year and on:	annual exam and continue to perform blood titer tests for antibodies to parvo and distemper yearly. DAP is only administered if immunity is low.

If you live in an area with a high risk of exposure, consider doing the vaccines that are recommended under those circumstances. For instance, in a high deer-tick area, you might consider the Lyme vaccine.

Note: The manufacturer's recommended vaccine protocol for the three-year DAP vaccine is to give it at eight weeks and twelve weeks, and then every three years. You can choose to do the blood titer test for parvo and distemper instead, and only revaccinate if the immunity is low.

Your veterinarian may recommend that you revaccinate, or provide a booster shot, on an annual basis for distemper and parvo. However, this may not be necessary. We suggest that you request a blood titer test to measure your dog's antibody levels for parvo and distemper. Titers measure the level of antibodies present in the dog. If the antibodies are adequate, the dog has adequate protection from the diseases. Therefore, no vaccine is needed to boost this protection.

If you run blood titer tests on a yearly basis, you will most likely find your dog's levels of distemper and parvo antibodies are adequate for three to four years following a vaccination, and will not require revaccination for several years.

When the dog is approaching middle age, blood work can be done as a screening test to be sure the dog is aging without complications. This will provide a baseline as well to measure future blood work by. This is a much better approach to protecting your dog than just automatically vaccinating year after year.

What to Do Before and After Vaccinations

If you decide that giving vaccinations is the best option for you, there are things you can do that will help your dog have the best possible outcome. First, you'll want to make sure your dog's immune system is boosted through nutritional support. You'll need to increase your dog's supplements a couple of weeks prior to vaccination. Immediately following the vaccinations, you can administer homeopathic remedies that will help your dog recover quickly and detoxify his body simultaneously. More than one vaccine should not be given at the same time with the exception of kennel cough which is administered orally.

To help to offset any side effects that could be caused by giving rabies vaccine, we suggest you give the homeopathic remedy Lyssin (200C). This is a remedy made from the saliva of a rabid dog. Homeopathy works with the premise that "like cures like." To offset any negative effects of the parvo/distemper vaccines, we suggest Thuja occidentalis (200C), which is made from the bark of the tree. This remedy provides specific actions on the body's urinary system, skin, and spinal cord. It is considered one of the most commonly used remedies to restore the body to health if any problems occur after vaccination. The appropriate remedy can be given orally two hours after the vaccine has been given. This can also help take away any potential long-term negative effects of the vaccine. Have these remedies on hand before bringing your dog in for vaccinations. Both

Lyssin and Thuja occidentalis come in pellet form and can be administered separately either by placing three pellets directly into the dog's mouth or by diluting pellets in ½ glass of bottled or filtered water and adding to the dog's water or food.

Some of the worst problems occur after the rabies vaccination has been given to a young dog (usually between three and four months old). Though rare, specific problems the rabies vaccine can cause are seizures, aggressive behavior in a dog that was previously very affectionate, or swelling of the face and body. Holistic veterinarians view these problems that arise after the rabies vaccine as most difficult to treat because they were caused by a man-made product.

Why Vaccines Are Not Harmless

Many studies by caring and concerned veterinarians have found that overvaccinating (with yearly vaccinations) could be the culprit behind the diseases becoming so apparent in our dogs today. Their overuse is causing what has been coined as "vaccinosis" in our dogs. Vaccinosis, according to Dr. Richard Pitcairn, is the expression of chronic disease brought on by vaccination.

The most common diseases on the rise in our dogs today are allergies, arthritis, cancer, and diabetes. Some of the statistics that are not being talked about as readily to the public suggest that allergies can be triggered by vaccinations. For instance, specific studies have proved that dogs that were genetically predisposed to develop dermatitis (inflammatory skin condition where there is much itching and which can lead to "hot spots" or deeper skin infections if left untreated) contracted this particular skin condition only if they were vaccinated before being exposed to the allergen. Interestingly, if a

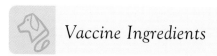

Vaccine Ingredients

Vaccines contain so-called preservatives. Thimerosal, a commonly used preservative, is made up of ethyl mercury, a highly toxic metal that affects the neurological system in humans and dogs. It can also affect the immune system—the very thing vaccinations are supposed to enhance or protect—affect motor skills, and create behavioral problems, and it has even been linked to autism in humans.

Along with that, this metal is second only to uranium as the most poisonous substance to humankind. It does not leave the body through the normal elimination process but rather is cumulative. As it accumulates, the body will eventually become so toxic that the immune system will not be able to handle it, and it sets up the perfect environment for disease to thrive in.

Another very toxic ingredient commonly found in vaccines is aluminum, more commonly referred to as formaldehyde. Formaldehyde is used in science to preserve body parts. Ethylene glycol, what we know as antifreeze, is also an ingredient in vaccines. Many dogs die each year from drinking antifreeze, yet it is also a primary ingredient in vaccines.

Common Effects of Vaccines on Dogs

• Increased aggression, particularly with annual vaccinations

• Increased scratching and itching, often at the vaccine site

• Restless and irritable behavior, particularly with annual vaccinations

dog has not been vaccinated, the chances of a dormant skin condition or dermatitis developing are slim to none, particularly if the dog's immune system is fully supported through proper feeding and nutrition.

In dogs with arthritis, particles of vaccine have been found in the actual bone of the dogs studied. In dogs with cancer, the cancer formed or started at the site on the body where the vaccine was administered. Many autoimmune disorders in our dogs, such as diabetes, Cushing's disease (a disease of the pituitary or adrenal glands), and thyroid disease, are also being directly linked to the actual vaccine administered. Studies have shown that some dogs are genetically predisposed to suffer fatal reactions to vaccines, or to develop fatal diseases as a direct result of being vaccinated. Effectively, vaccinating yearly is contributing more disease rather than preventing it as was originally thought.

Seizure Side Effect?

According to his caregiver, Ollie was a happy and healthy German shepherd puppy of four months of age when he received his first rabies vaccine. The very next day he had a seizure, and then had repeated seizures weekly for months. Sadly, his condition could not be controlled with the standard conventional treatment of phenobarbital and KBr (potassium bromide). The caregiver came to see me about this problem when Ollie was eight months old. Unfortunately, no matter how hard I tried to cure this dog with homeopathy, I could not. The caregivers and the dog suffered for many years with this problem.

The Cause of Aggression?

Pavel, the cutest brown-and-white Cavalier King Charles, came to see me starting from the time he was a puppy. We did all the prescribed puppy shots, and he was fine. At four months old, he received the rabies vaccine. One month after getting the rabies vaccine, this very sweet, adorable puppy started biting his caregiver whenever she put his food down. He then started biting at her whenever she went to put his harness on. We tried conventional medicines to try to calm him down, but they didn't help. Marie, his caregiver, asked me to try treating him with homeopathy. Some remedies helped for short periods of time but the dog would revert back to his aggressive self. The caregivers lost patience with the homeopathic treatment and now just suffer with this dog's aggressive behavior. He is only two years old.

Feel Like You've Been Left in the Dark?

You may be wondering if this is all public record, why all veterinarians aren't telling us vaccinations are not the best path to preventative health. Why do they continue to insist on annual boosters? Traditional veterinarians teach and most believe that by practicing traditional vaccination-oriented disease prevention they are providing excellent care for your dog. There is also, unfortunately, the element of revenue they receive from administering vaccines, which is a large part of the veterinary business.

This is a very controversial issue in the veterinary community and has been for the last few years.

Most homeopathic and homeopathic-complementary veterinarians take the approach of doing what's best for the individual patient not just what's considered standard. This may be true partly because homeopathic veterinarians started out in traditional medicine and then expanded their studies to include holistic care. That education furthered their knowledge in caring for the entire animal rather than just treating symptoms. What is important for you is that you choose a veterinarian who is open to having a discussion with you about these issues, a veterinarian who is open to hearing your concerns and will not force you into giving vaccines, and most importantly that you educate yourself as your dog's medical advocate to ask the right questions.

"A practice that was started years ago and that lacks scientific validity or verification is annual revaccinations. Almost without exception there is no immunologic requirement for annual revaccination. Immunity to viruses persists for years or for the life of the dog. The practice of annual vaccination in our opinion should be considered of questionable efficacy unless it is used as a mechanism to provide an annual physical examination or is required by law (i.e., certain states require annual revaccination for rabies)."

Excerpted from Current Veterinary Therapy XI, written by Tom Phillips and Ronal Shultz for conventional veterinarians

The Status Quo

Once immunity to a disease exists in your dog, that immunity will extend for the life of your dog. Although immunity most likely exists with the first set of puppy shots, we are still told to vaccinate annually. There are several reasons for this.

First, veterinarians are taught that annual vaccines are appropriate and save lives by preventing disease. Second, the vaccine manufacturers themselves have dictated the frequency of the vaccine protocols. Because the manufacturers tested their products on only a one-year basis, they are allowed to put forth only an annual protocol for most vaccines. Testing the vaccines for a longer period would incur added expense, so until recently, the one-year protocol was standard. (Recently, one vaccine manufacturer came out with a new distemper/parvo vaccine that is good for three years, showing that progress is being made.) Third, veterinarians feel it is best to follow the manufacturer's recommendation for vaccine effectiveness. As you can see, the decision to administer vaccines annually is largely driven by the manufacturers.

Changing Perspective

In the last few years, many veterinarians have conducted their own research studies on vaccines. Many of these were conventional feline practitioners, worried about the increased incidence of tumors growing at the sites of vaccines. They set up studies that exposed animals, for up to three years, to the diseases that they were vaccinated for three years prior. The veterinarians found that these animals (mostly cats) had immunity for the entire three-year period. They then made recommendations in the veterinary journals to revise cats' vaccine protocols based on these findings, and suggested vaccinating cats no more than every three years with the feline viral rhinotracheitis/calicivirus/panleukopenia (FVRCP) vaccine.

The canine practitioners soon followed with comparable studies, and found the same results. They also recommended dogs be vaccinated no more than every three years for canine distemper and parvo virus.

Many conventional veterinarians are now using a new three-year vaccine. It is a modified live virus vaccine called Continuum DAP (distemper/adenovirus/parvo virus). This vaccine contains attenuated strains of three canine bioagents: distemper, parvo virus, and adenovirus.

Conventional veterinarians who, in practice, followed manufacturers' directions, are now able to vaccinate every three years with an accepted vaccine labeled for this purpose.

How You Can Change the Way Your Dog Is Vaccinated

Many changes happen due to the demand of pet owners. You can control what the veterinarian gives your dog, and you can make a big difference.

1. Request that your veterinarian use only the three-year DAP vaccine.

2. Ask for the intranasal bordetella (kennel cough) vaccine instead of the injectable one. Question your veterinarian's reasons for suggesting any other vaccine.

3. Be sure you request the three-year rabies vaccine after the first year's booster. Be sure the veterinarian marks that it is not due again until three years from the date given. (Some veterinarians give the three-year vaccine but put down that it is renewable in two years.) There is no such thing as a rabies vaccine that is manufactured with only two years of efficacy. They are labeled for either one year or three years. And if your veterinarian won't listen to you, take your dog to a different veterinarian, one who is more open to your suggestions.

Travel and Vaccine Requirements

Many people travel a lot and have to leave their dogs at kennels. Most kennels will not allow you to board your dog without being current on vaccines. Not only that, but kennels are noisy, strange places where your dog could potentially be exposed to bacteria and viruses. If you decide not to give annual vaccinations, boarding at a kennel is simply not the best option.

Fortunately, for those who don't want to do annual vaccines, a fast-rising industry is pet sitting. Pet sitters will come to your home and not only play with and feed your dog, but administer medications or supplements as well. Your dog is comfortable in his own home with his own toys, and he gets to "stay on the job" protecting the family home.

If you are forced to board your dog away from home, please check the kennel out well before leaving your dog there. Some kennels are being educated by veterinarians about the distemper and parvo titers being adequate for protection, and will accept these blood tests as evidence of immunity for your dog. It may be possible for a nonvaccinated dog to stay at a kennel, though hiring a pet sitter might still be a better option.

If you are flying with your dog, most airlines require a health certificate written within ten days of flying, and a current rabies vaccine certificate. There are some airlines that do not require this. It is suggested that you check in advance of your trip to see if your airline is one that requires these certificates.

Another situation in which you may need proof of rabies vaccination and a current health certificate is when traveling over borders. Please take this into consideration when planning a trip with your dog.

Moving On

We hope this chapter gave you a good alternative view of the vaccine issue. This is a very controversial issue in the field of veterinary medicine. Please see our recommended vaccine protocol, on page 75. Again, we suggest you find a veterinarian who is willing to have an honest and open conversation with you about these issues. As veterinarians, we all take an oath upon graduation to "do no harm." I believe all veterinarians want to uphold that oath and will listen to you and work with you around this issue to do that.

Chapter Six

Check-ups: Health and Age

You want to keep your little furry friend healthy and happy for her entire life—that's a given. So how can you do that? One of the most important things is to schedule annual visits with your veterinarian. Here are our recommendations for veterinary visits with dogs of different ages and with different issues.

Puppy

As soon as you get your puppy, schedule a visit with your veterinarian to make sure that all systems are working well and that your puppy is getting a healthy start. The veterinarian will give your puppy a thorough checkup from nose to toes.

Bring a small fecal (stool) sample with you on your first visit so your veterinarian can check for internal parasites (worms in the stool). Parasites are often passed to the puppy in utero (while the fetus is still in the uterus) by the mother. Worms can cause vomiting and diarrhea in your dog. More importantly, these worms can be passed to children inadvertently and cause serious problems in children. So making sure your dog is worm-free is very important to the health of you, your dog, and your entire family.

Intestinal worms can easily be treated with medication. In chapter eight, we'll be discussing natural ways you can eliminate parasites from your dog or puppy.

If there seems to be excessive discharge in your puppy's ears, your veterinarian will also check for ear mites. Ear mites are very contagious to all animals in your home; however, they are not a problem to humans. Your veterinarian will discuss good puppy care with you as well. In general, puppies should be kept inside away from other dogs until after sixteen weeks of age and when all vaccines, should you decide to go this route, have been administered. If you adopt an older dog, we still suggest a visit to the veterinarian for all the above reasons.

If you have a puppy, be prepared for several visits every three weeks until all the vaccines are finished. When the puppy is six months of age, it should be spayed or neutered. After that first year, annual visits are suggested. This is usually done a year from the rabies vaccine. Yearly visits are recommended so that you and your veterinarian can have an ongoing record of your dog's weight and general health. Yearly tests for heartworm disease and fecal exams for parasites are usually performed at these annual visits as well. Any vaccines, if needed, will also be given at this visit. (See chapter five for more on vaccines.)

A Special Note on Worms

If you choose to use holistic methods to take care of worms, it is very important that you test your dog's stool frequently to be sure the worms have been effectively and completely eliminated. A homeopathic remedy known to eliminate worms is Cina. You can give Cina 30C pellets once a day for three days. Repeat this same treatment again after three weeks, and repeat the fecal test after administering the second treatment. If the worms are still present, I would suggest using the conventional treatment as prescribed by your veterinarian.

That said, with children present, it may be safest for you to use natural products in deworming your dog. In chapter eight, we discuss this in detail, but one form that works well is using food-grade diatomaceous earth, which can also be used in your yard to remove pests.

Important: There are certain intestinal parasites that can be transmitted from a dog to children. If you have children, please discuss parasite control with your veterinarian, and check your dog's stools frequently to be sure your pet is parasite free.

Middle Age

Depending on the breed and size of your dog, middle age may come at different times. Generally, larger dogs have a shorter life span than smaller dogs.

We recommend full blood work and urine analysis when your dog is considered middle age. For many dogs, this can be at seven to ten years old. This is to have a baseline should the dog ever become ill in the future. It's also a way to catch any problems while they are in the early stages of developing, because many times, dogs won't show symptoms until they are very ill.

We recommend a full blood and urine analysis every two to three years after that, even if your dog is healthy. Other visits to the veterinarian will be determined by your dog's overall health. Many dogs stay very healthy until they reach seniority. These dogs and caregivers luckily may visit their veterinarian only once a year for a long time. Other dogs unluckily get recurrent problems (diarrhea, ear infections, skin problems, allergies, etc.). For these problems, you may be at the veterinarian's office more frequently. We recommend that you address these problems as soon as you notice them. Waiting more than a day usually results in the problems' getting worse.

Any eye problem or ear problem normally requires immediate attention. These types of problems usually do not resolve on their own. Of course, you can try the alternatives mentioned in this book before going to the veterinarian, or try going to a holistic veterinarian—just do something to alleviate this problem within the first day or two after noticing it. Please don't wait until after normal veterinary office hours to contact your veterinarian. There will always be more options for treatment if you contact your veterinarian when his or her office is open. Many people, for some reason, wait until Sunday and then panic and find themselves at an emergency clinic, working with a veterinarian who doesn't know them or their dog, doesn't have the dog's past veterinary history or know the current problems, and charges two to three times what you might have paid at your regular veterinarian during regular office hours.

Dental Care

"Doggie breath" is often something people assume is normal for dogs, but it isn't. A dog that is fed correctly and has clean white teeth should not have smelly dog breath. There are a lot of factors that can contribute to the bad breath. While few dental conditions are life threatening, there are problems that can arise in your dog's overall health if you do not attend to her dental care on a regular basis. Just like humans, if the teeth are not cleaned and kept plaque-free, other diseases can crop up that may be life threatening.

If your dog's teeth are dirty and full of crusted plaque, the gums can become infected. This infection can spread to the heart and other internal organs in your dog, causing potentially serious problems. Sometimes the teeth become so severely encrusted that an abscess can occur in the mouth, something that is extremely painful and can cause your dog to stop eating.

Dogs can lose many of their teeth just because regular dental care was not performed. On the upside, if you feed your dog a natural diet, this normally won't be an issue for your dog. A natural diet will include bone, which will help keep that smile pearly white and healthy.

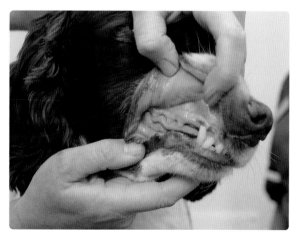

Veterinarians regularly check your dog's teeth as part of her yearly exam. Healthy teeth and gums are critical to your dog's overall health. Just as in humans, dogs can get periodontal disease, particularly when fed a kibble-based diet.

You can purchase toothpaste that is specially formulated for dogs or make your own using water and baking soda to form a thick paste, then sprinkle in a drop of natural sweetner such as stevia, available at health food stores. You can also add a sprinkle of salt for its antiseptic and abrasive qualities. Place the toothpaste on a soft-bristled brush sized for your dog's mouth. Gently brush from the gum line downward. Brush both sides of the hard-to-reach teeth in the very front and very back. Allow breaks for your dog to breath, lick, relax, and swallow, and keep the sessions short and fun.

For today's dog, the bad breath and tartar problems stem from an improper diet that is the equivalent of too much junk food and lack of dental hygiene. Much of the pet food on the market is not much better than a regular diet of candy. (We will delve deeper into this subject in the next chapter.) By doing regular maintenance checks on your dog's teeth along with your other grooming tasks, such as ear cleaning, brushing, and bathing, you will be able to avoid most serious dental problems. Combine that with a natural diet, and your dog should have clean, healthy, white teeth for life.

The key is to keep that plaque from starting in the first place. Having a dental cleaning performed on your dog every year at your veterinarian's is not only expensive but an added risk to your dog since your dog will need to be put under anesthesia for this procedure. Natural regular maintenance is the best choice for your dog and your pocketbook.

Mental Health Issues

Many of you reading this section might think, "Mental health issues in a dog?" Yes, believe it or not, dogs have issues just like we do, although the big difference is they can't tell us what is wrong.

Dogs suffer from a variety of mental disorders such as separation, social, and noise anxiety and also obsessive compulsive disorder (OCD). Most dog caregivers have probably heard of, if not experienced, separation anxiety in dogs. A lot of rescues or formerly abused dogs can suffer from this disorder, as can dogs that were not properly socialized as puppies.

Your dog will show his anxiety in a number of ways, and most likely in ways that will leave you pondering dog caregivership. However, since our dogs rely on us for all their provisions, it is up to us as responsible dog caregivers to not only recognize our dog's problems, but to take the necessary steps to help our dogs overcome these problems and to relieve the stressful situations that are aggravating these problems.

Often, if a dog is stressed or suffering from one of the above disorders, he will show us obvious signs. Once we learn to recognize the signs, we can then move forward to help our dogs overcome the problem. Simple signs of anxiety include shivering uncontrollably; excessive drooling; heavy panting; lots of yawning, moaning, and whining; excessive barking; and even refusal to move. Some of these signs can also be associated with pain or a medical condition. We recommend always having a checkup with your veterinarian to make sure there is no medical problem before assuming it is just a behavioral or emotional issue.

You'll probably notice these behaviors actively when you take your dog to visit the veterinarian. That is normal. Fun things don't often happen at the veterinarian's office, and your dog will anticipate the "white coat syndrome" humans experience when we go to the doctor. If, however, your dog exhibits some or all of these symptoms whenever you go to leave your house then you probably do have a problem that needs to be addressed.

Your first step should be to take your dog to see a holistic veterinarian. They can often help to resolve these separation anxiety issues gently, using homeopathic supplements and other holistic treatments. (See Appendix C, page 165 for more information.)

Separation Anxiety

If you come home to chewed-up furniture and personal belongings; elimination messes on your floors; trenches dug in your yards, gardens, rugs, or floors; or you hear your dog howling loudly enough to shake buildings, your dog is most likely suffering from separation anxiety. This seems to be one of the most common mental health issues in dogs. Dogs are pack animals, and that means they are not meant to be left alone. If your dog is the only dog in the household, you become his pack.

Different dogs do different things to show you how they feel. Some become very destructive of your things, others howl and moan, while still others hunker down for the long haul to wait for your return. The bottom line is that they are all waiting to be reunited with their pack, and that means you. This problem may be more evident in dogs that were formerly abandoned, but it can happen even in a dog that was well raised. The solution lies with you and the choices you make to remedy the situation.

Regular exercise is a must for a happy, healthy dog. Your dog needs a daily dose of exercise to keep his body fit, his mind alert, and his spirit energized. This is especially important for the sporting and herding dogs.

Lurcher and Keeshond

What often happens is that caregivers with dogs who have this problem will reinforce the problem by some actions they actually think are helping. For instance, you get ready to leave (your dog knows the signs that say you are leaving), so you start making a big to-do about it. You promise to return soon, you hug and kiss and keep talking to your dog, delaying your departure while trying to reassure your dog of your return. By doing this, you are only reinforcing the problem. The more you try to reassure your dog as you try to slip out the door, the more you tell him he has something to worry about. A better way to handle leaving is simply to say good-bye and leave.

One way to overcome this problem is to leave for short time periods and return again. Maybe on days off from work, you can leave for fifteen minutes and then return. Go for longer periods of time each time until your dog comes to realize that you are not going to abandon her.

Leaving your dog home with some great mind-stimulating toys can also help. Challenging toys are ones that make your dog think or try to get something out of the toy, like a piece of food inside a KONG toy (a toy with a hollow center). These types of approaches can keep your dog stress-free and both of you happy.

Social Anxiety

Another mental health issue in dogs is social anxiety. This is why socializing your dog as a puppy is so important. Most dogs that suffer from this disorder do so as a direct result of improper socialization as puppies. By following the steps outlined here, you and your dog can avoid this disorder altogether.

The very nature of dogs is social, meaning they need interaction with other dogs and humans. Without social interaction, your dog's natural disposition is being suppressed. When dogs are deprived of social interaction, they can develop mental problems and even become a danger to humans. Dogs with social anxiety are most likely dogs that have been left alone for most of their lives, and/or tied up outside with little or no social interaction.

Trust is such an important issue; we can't stress it enough. If you gain your dog's trust through the proper approach, he'll love and trust you for life. Do this by interacting with him as a member of your family and taking him out in public where he can be around other dogs and humans. Taking your dog for regular rides in the car will help him get used to being in public and in different situations. This also helps him build confidence and learn how to behave as a good canine citizen in public.

Dogs want and need boundaries, but they can't know what those boundaries are unless you teach them from a viewpoint they'll understand. In other words, you do need to know something about how dogs think in order to communicate effectively with them. By training your dog properly, preferably with a reputable dog trainer, you are going to learn how to train your dog in a way he will understand, thus avoiding potentially dangerous mental problems such as social anxiety. Many veterinarians, dog trainers, and doggie day-care centers in large cities offer puppy play groups. These are for younger dogs that would benefit from socialization with other healthy puppies.

Investing the time in training and socialization when your dog is young will pay off greatly with his devotion to you in later years.

German Shorthaired Pointers

Sensitivity to Noise

Another source of anxiety is unexpected noise. Have you ever heard a police siren going off and it seems as though all the dogs in the neighborhood decided to join in the chorus? Well, often that is just because the sound is extraordinarily loud to dogs and it hurts their ears. For other dogs, however, it is more than that. They can become extremely frightened by any loud sounds from car horns and backfires, firecrackers, sirens, thunder, and gunshots. To them, anything loud is a reason to panic and go into fight-or-flight mode. That can be a very dangerous situation for your dog, particularly if he runs out into a street full of traffic.

While this disorder may seem hopeless or overwhelming, the good news is that it can be overcome with patience and due diligence on your part. The key to overcoming this problem is to desensitize your dog to these sounds. While you don't want to go out and abruptly immerse your dog right in the midst of the noisiest, loudest sounds, by consistently exposing him to these sounds in small doses, your dog can overcome this disorder.

There are also some good natural products you can use to help your dog remain calm and not react to loud noises in your absence. Flower essences and essential oils can help your dog learn to associate certain smells and feelings with calmness, so that you eventually won't need to use them except in extreme situations. These flower essences and essential oils will not have the side effects that many medications have, so they are good additions to your natural care arsenal. (See chapter nine for more information on this approach).

Moving On

As we mentioned, an average healthy dog should have a yearly appointment with the veterinarian. You may also find that there are other times of the year when you need to go see the veterinarian for a special test (for example, a heartworm test in April or May). For older dogs with ongoing problems such as heart disease, hypothyroid, or allergies, we suggest veterinary visits every six months. There may be tests that can be done to assess the effectiveness of a medication, which will help the veterinarian regulate these medications accordingly. However, it is your responsibility to take care of and observe your dog on a daily basis.

Remember, the key to a healthy dog is to care for the whole dog and not just the parts. That means caring for the mind, body, and spirit of your dog. Sound mental health can make a lot of difference in your dog's physical health, and vice versa. In the following chapters, we'll explore the different things you can do and what to avoid in order to maintain this picture of optimal health in your dog. Consult the Doggie Checklist Calendar on the following spread for an at-a-glance guide to daily caregiving.

Doggie Checklist Calendar

ON A DAILY BASIS

Eating habits: normal / increased / decreased

Note:

Urination: normal / increased / decreased

Note:

Defecation: normal / increased / decreased

Note:

Water intake: normal / increased / decreased

Note:

Temperature: normal / overly hot / overly cold

Note:

Level of energy: normal / increased / decreased

Note:

Skin and coat: normal / too oily / too dry / flaky / rash / lumps

Note:

Mouth (teeth): normal / discolored / tartar buildup / odor

Note:

Mouth (gums): normal / too pale / too dark / dry / inflamed

Note:

Eyes: normal / discharge / lids sticking together / inflamed

Note:

Teeth: ate raw bones / brushed

Note:

Coat: brushed (daily for long-haired dogs) / checked for lumps or bumps

Note:

ON A WEEKLY BASIS

Weight: normal / underweight / overweight
Note:

Ears: normal / waxy / dirty / inflamed
Note:

Nails: normal / brittle / bleeding
Note:

Teeth and gums: normal / buildup/ need cleaning / gums bleeding
Note:

Coat: brushed (weekly for short-haired dogs) / checked for lumps or bumps
Note:

ON A MONTHLY BASIS

Coat and skin: normal / odorous / oily / dry / flaky / has rash / needs a bath
Note:

Medication: normal reaction / no reaction / diarrhea / vomiting / more or less energy
Note:

Nails: normal / need clipping
Note:

Mouth: normal / growth / discoloration
Note:

Chapter Seven

Food and Nutrition

"If one is sick and desires healing, it is of prime importance that the true cause of the sickness be discovered." —Andrew Murray, writer and pastor

The basis for good health in our dogs is diet and the key to good health is prevention. The more natural and fresh the diet, the more nutrients are available for our dogs' bodies to use in building a good immune system, which will then ward off illness and disease.

As we stated in chapter five, annual vaccines are contributing in large part to the decline in the health of our dogs. The second or equal contributor to this decline in health is what we feed our dogs. The three main options for feeding a dog:

1. Commercially packaged dog food
2. Home-cooked diet
3. Raw meat and bones

In this chapter, we'll give you the pros and cons of each choice of what to feed your dog—providing you with the information you need to make your own choice. If your choice is commercial food, we will tell you what to avoid in your commercial food choice to help you to choose the one with the most nutritional value.

Commercial Pet Food

In 1890, the first known commercial pet food came into existence. It was a wet food (canned food) made of horse meat. Dry food, or what we now know as kibble, didn't become popular until the 1950s. This is an extremely popular choice for feeding, especially because of its convenience and price.

We've been taught by our veterinarians and the pet food industry that feeding our dogs commercial food and no human food is the best way to keep them healthy. This, however, is contrary to a dog's natural method of eating. If you choose the commercial food method, you'll need to add supplements, probiotics, and innate enzymes to the food to maintain the nutrient level best for a dog's good health. In the next section,

Labrador Retriever

we'll discuss other, and in our opinion, better ways of feeding, but for now, let's look at ingredients to avoid in commercial dog food should you decide this is the best feeding method for your lifestyle.

Ingredients

Some of the things you'll most often see listed on the label of your kibble or canned food are different types of grains. Dogs, however, do not fare well on grains because they are carnivores and their bodies weren't made to digest grains. The reason grains are

The Cost of Kibble

In the long run, you will pay far more in veterinary costs and experience more behavioral problems in your dog by feeding him a lower quality food just for the sake of convenience and price. If you start out with natural feeding, you'll save money and have a healthier, happier dog.

Sample Ingredient List for Commercial Dog Food

Lamb, brewer's rice, oatmeal, corn gluten meal, poultry by-product meal, whole-grain corn, animal fat preserved with mixed tocopherols, nonfat yogurt, dicalcium phosphate, calcium carbonate, animal digest, potassium chloride, malted barley flour, salt, choline chloride, brewer's dried yeast, zinc sulfate, vitamin E supplement, ferrous sulfate, L-Lysine mono-hydrochloride, manganese sulfate, niacin, vitamin A supplement, calcium pantothenate, thiamine mononitrate, copper sulfate, riboflavin supplement, vitamin B12 supplement, pyridoxine hydrochloride, garlic oil, folic acid, vitamin D3 supplement, calcium iodate, biotin, menadione sodium bisulfate complex, sodium selenite.

added to commercial dog foods is that they are cheap and your dog can survive on them for a while before health problems begin to manifest.

Meat is often listed as the first ingredient in commercial dog food, which seems healthy at first glance. Unfortunately this meat has been cooked for so long that the nutritional value is gone, and the beneficial fats and enzymes are no longer present. Once you cook the meat beyond 180°F (85°C), you have lost most of the valuable ingredients your dog needs to be able to maintain optimal health.

We'd prefer that dog caregivers avoid kibble and canned food altogether, but since many people aren't ready to take the leap into cooked or raw feeding, here are some guidelines to help you make informed decisions for your dogs.

- Avoid commercial foods that have chemical preservatives such as butylated hydroxyanisole (BHT), butylated hydroxytoluene (BHA), or ethoxyquin, and choose those that have natural preservatives such as vitamin C, E, and mixed tocopherols. Tocopherols have a very potent form of natural vitamin E activity and are very often used as a natural preservative.

- Try to avoid canned food altogether. It consists of the worst junk parts of dead animals, along with poor-quality grains packaged in such a way as to sound appealing. It also is made to appear as though you are feeding meat to your dog. Really, it's mostly grain, by-products, and preservatives with flavoring added. Added salt is another common ingredient (also found in kibble). Most canned food also contains propylene glycol, which is a nice word for a petroleum by-product and very dangerous to your dog's health.

- Store kibble in an airtight container in a dry environment. All kibble contains storage mites, and those mites love humid conditions and mold. According to Steve Brown and Beth Taylor, in their book *See Spot Live Longer,* "Recent studies in peer-reviewed veterinary studies worldwide show that the consumption of the carcasses of storage mites that are in the grains used in dog foods may be a major contributing factor in symptoms of allergies in dogs."

This is how it happens: The mites like to eat the grains, particularly the broken grains used in dog foods, and have a special fondness for the mold found on the grains. When the molds are being eaten by the mites, they secrete deadly mycotoxins (mycotoxins are chemicals secreted by toxic mold), and when the grain is processed, all of this ends up in the kibble. Even worse, storage mites can also contaminate the food in your home. (Note that *all* commercial packaged animal foods contain some form of mold.)

Common Preservatives

According to Sandra Brigola, editor and publisher of *Canine Health Naturally* newsletter, the stored grains that are used in commercial pet foods "... are sprayed with ethoxyquin (a toxic preservative), and moldy grains that have mycotoxins, aflatoxin, or fusarium molds, are hard to destroy. The allowable level in pet foods is 1.0 ppm (parts per million) [*Authors' note:* this is in reference to levels of mycotoxins allowable by the Food and Drug Administration]. The way that pet food manufacturers get around this is by mixing grains with higher levels of mycotoxins with grains of lesser levels; hopefully to reduce the higher levels."

- Try to avoid grains as much as possible. Your dog will live a much healthier and longer life if you will leave the grains out of his diet. When you are looking to purchase a commercial dog food, make sure that the grains are one of the last ingredients rather than one of the first. Always avoid any dog food that has corn in it. Dogs cannot digest corn, and over time, your dog's body will begin to get sick from it. Dogs can also have allergic reactions to wheat, soy, and rice. If you decide to choose kibble as your feeding method, try finding one that does not contain those ingredients. Another problem with grains is that they usually contain residue from the chemical fertilizers and pesticides that were applied to them in the field. Dogs can also be allergic to these chemicals (see chapter twelve for more information on environmental toxins).

- Choose a food that does not contain any by-products. *By-product* is a fancy word for everything that really should be tossed on the slaughterhouse floor and is not fit for human or dog consumption. By-products can include beaks, feathers, feet, diseased animal parts—just about everything that should be thrown out.

- Be very selective in the foods you purchase, and read the labels closely. There are some fairly decent commercially packaged dog foods; many are dehydrated and organic and come in sealed containers. Remember, though, that all packaged dry foods—no matter how premium they may be—contain storage mites.

- Add cooked meat to the kibble. You can also add in some cooked or steamed pureed vegetables and yogurt to enhance your dog's kibble.

Echinacea   **Garlic**   **Ginger**

- Make sure your dog is getting a daily supplement, preferably a whole food one, along with some added digestive enzymes. There are many forms and brands of supplements and enzymes you can give your dog. Be selective in choosing those that do not have preservatives or synthetic ingredients. We have some excellent resources for you in the back of the book.

Never mix cooked and raw meat. Cooked meat takes a much longer time to digest and raw meat is digested rapidly. Mixing them can confuse the enzyme process in your dog.

- Provide probiotics in the form of organic yogurt with live cultures, or purchase them as supplements in capsule or powder form. Probiotics are the good bacteria in your dog's intestines that help him digest certain foods and manufacture vitamins. Kibble does not contain any probiotics, so you will need to provide your dog with them.

- Add herbs to your dog's diet. Some good ones to include are ginger for motion sickness and burdock for allergies. See page 130 for more on herbs and their uses.

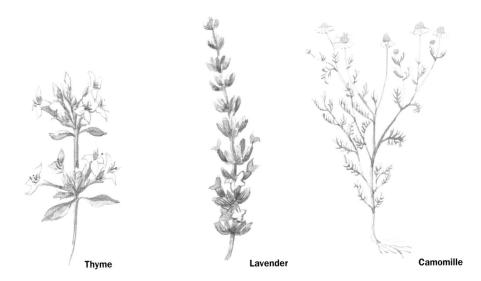

Thyme   **Lavender**   **Camomille**

Need More Convincing?

Because commercially packaged foods are usually so laden with grains and other undesirable ingredients, your dog will have more frequent and larger stools. The bigger the stools, the fewer nutrients are being assimilated into your dog's body. All the junk in commercial food will eventually take its toll on your dog's body, leading to a decline in health. He'll also have a more offensive body odor and doggy breath when fed a kibble-based diet.

Making a Change in Diet

Whenever you change your dog's diet, whether adding something new or subtracting something, always do it slowly. Your dog's digestive system needs time to adjust to a change. By making this change gradually over time, let's say two to three weeks, you should eliminate any potential for his having side effects such as a change in his stools. Making this change slowly will allow both of you to get used to this new way of feeding. It will also allow you to assess if it really is the way to go for both of you. If you choose not to change your dog's feeding, consider adding some of the supplements and other things suggested in the next section to enrich your dog's diet and health.

Home-Cooked Diets

The next method of feeding is a cooked diet. This method of feeding is far better than feeding commercially packaged dog food because your dog isn't getting all the fillers found in commercial food—he is actually eating pure food. You also won't need to feed as much as you would with kibble.

There is such a wide variety of recipes and ways to do this, and you'll want to choose a method that best fits your lifestyle. Many people will combine pureed fresh vegetables, meat, and eggs, and then bake the entire mixture. Or you can just choose to focus on meat and bones. It is also very convenient, as you can purchase everything right in the grocery store where you shop for your own food. You can make a fancy cooked diet for your dog, or a simple one. While you may think this sounds funny, your dog will really appreciate it.

Whatever you choose, you won't need to cook the food very long (unlike how we cook for ourselves). Dogs are bacteria machines, and because they have short intestines designed for carnivores, bacteria don't have time to incubate inside them like they do in humans. Therefore, home-cooked dog food is relatively easy and quick to prepare.

Many people who prepare cooked diets for their dogs will prepare enough for a week at a time, and then freeze the food. You can package daily portions of food in freezer bags or containers, freeze them, and then thaw each day's portion to room temperature before feeding it to your dog. The trick here is figuring out how much food to feed your dog each day. This will require a bit of experimentation and determination on your part to make sure you are giving your dog his required nutrition each day. The key is always to "know thy dog."

Never give your dog cooked meat bones. They are brittle and can splinter, causing internal damage when passing through the intestine. You can give your dog raw bones, however, as that is the best way for dogs to receive needed minerals and enzymes.

The Downside to a Home-Cooked Diet

One of the downsides to this diet is that many of the good enzymes and probiotics found in food are killed off during the cooking process. Anytime we cook food over 180°F (85°C), enzymes and probiotics are destroyed in the process. Because beneficial enzymes and probiotics may be cooked out, you'll want to supplement your dog's diet with a daily whole food supplement, or add enzymes and probiotics.

Another downside is you will spend more time preparing your dog's food than you do with kibble, and it can be more expensive. While it may take a bit more of your time and cost more, in the long run, you'll be saving money on veterinarian bills because your dog will be much healthier.

When feeding a home-cooked diet, it is important to do your research and "know thy dog" to determine his needs. Part of feeding natural foods is understanding that your dog is an individual, and each dog will be a bit different in his nutritional needs.

Raw Diet

The third method of feeding is a raw food and bone diet, more commonly known as a BARF (Biologically Appropriate Raw Food), which will include a variety of different meats, bones, and even some vegetables, eggs, yogurt, and nuts, or SARF (Species Appropriate Raw Food), which excludes vegetables, eggs, and nuts. These methods of feeding are much closer to how a wild dog would eat, or how any dog would eat if given the choice. These diets are also the healthiest choice for your dog.

This feeding method is the most desirable, natural, and evolutionary for a dog to eat. Dogs are designed to digest and utilize raw meat, bones, and any other part of a prey animal's carcass. This includes meat, bone, fat, some vegetable material, and even the fur.

A diet consisting of primarily raw meat and bones will help your dog's body deal with or even eliminate many of the common ailments we've seen in dogs today. Hot spots, excessive shedding, flea infestations, parasites, bad teeth and gum problems, allergies, and degenerative diseases can all be attributed to poor nutrition and overvaccination. Many of these ailments we've come to accept as normal, but they can be avoided altogether with a proper natural diet.

While a raw diet has long been a common practice in Europe and other countries, it is still not readily accepted in the United States. European veterinarians commonly recommend a raw diet for dogs, while American veterinarians commonly recommend feeding kibble. The fear of feeding raw meat in the United States is usually due to concern over salmonella, e. coli, and parasites. As we stated earlier, dogs are bacteria machines, and their digestive systems are designed to handle raw meat. They are much more likely to get parasites or bacteria from sources such as another dog's feces or dirt rather than the human-grade meat you'll provide for them.

If you are concerned about the bacteria and parasites in raw meat, there are things you can do to counter any possible problems. Herbs, essential oils, or food-grade diatomaceous earth can all be effective with this (see chapter nine for more information).You can also freeze the meat and then thaw it out before feeding your dog, effectively killing most bacteria.

Benefits of a Raw Food Diet

Border Collie

- No bad body odor or breath

- Clean, white teeth (because of the bones he's eating)

- Small, dry stools (If you don't pick up your dog's waste daily, you may notice that some will just disintegrate right back into the soil, just like a wild dog's does.)

- Shiny, glossy coat

What Goes into a Raw Diet?

The best raw food diet consists of a variety of meats and raw bone. When switching to this diet, you can start out with chicken and slowly add in other meats. A dog can eat any part of the chicken, but chicken wings, backs, and necks are a very good start for your dog. You'll also want a ratio of one to one bone to meat, choosing meaty smaller bones verses big large bones with very little meat. Chicken and turkey necks, backs, and wings provide a near perfect bone to meat ratio. Feed your dog 35 to 40 percent meat, 10 percent organ meat, and 50 percent bone. Be careful not to feed your dog organ meat more than a couple of times a week, as it is too rich in vitamin A. Feed chicken livers with chicken, beef livers with beef, and so on, as this will mimic a natural wild diet. Feed your dog two to three percent of his body weight per day in either one or two meals per day.

Another excellent raw food to feed your dog is tripe. It is one of the most balanced "meats" to feed your dog. Yes, raw tripe may sound gross to us, but dogs love it. Make sure it is green tripe and not the bleached tripe you see in your grocery store. You'll have to get this tripe from a meat supplier or a butcher.

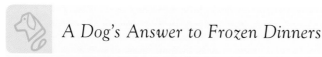

Freeze-dried packaged meat or natural dehydrated diets can be ordered from certain companies over the Internet or by phone and shipped to you for your convenience. These types of foods are made with human-grade ingredients. They have been gently dehydrated, removing only the water from the food, making shipping and storing easy. All of the other needed nutrients in the food remain intact and actually become highly concentrated as a result of the dehydration process. To rehydrate this food, you simply add warm water and allow the food to sit for about ten minutes. Many people who use this type of food add in some fresh meat and bone to give it the "yummy factor" for their dogs.

Keep in mind that these foods are usually fairly pricey, and you may even need to add some raw meat to balance your dog's diet. However, these freeze-dried or dehydrated packaged natural meat diets are very good alternatives to a kibble-based diet and are closer to a raw diet. You'll not need as much supplementation with these dehydrated or freeze-dried diets as you would when feeding a kibble diet.

Vegetarianism in Dogs: A Good Idea or Not?

Simply put, the answer is no. Why? Because dogs are carnivores. Carnivores are meat eaters, and meat is what they need to maintain optimal health.

There are some of you who may have already put your dog on a vegetarian diet, and you may see an improvement in certain conditions. This could be true just because most vegetarian diets are put together without by-products and other fillers such as those found in commercial dog food. Removing these things from your dog's diet alone may have improved his health. Vegetables can be added to any diet (pulverized for easier digestion), but dogs need meat for long-term overall health.

Labrador Retriever

A small percentage of dogs may be allergic to bee pollen. Therefore, if you choose to give this as a supplement, start with the smallest amount (1 grain) and then increase to a dose that would be appropriate for your size dog. Locally produced bee pollen is best.

Supplements

In most instances, supplements are a necessary part of a healthy dog's diet. Supplements can help your dog's immune system build up more quickly and become stronger, which is especially beneficial to overvaccinated dogs.

With so many undesirable substances in our meats and vegetables these days—including hormones, antibiotics, pesticides, and herbicides—your dog will need help, in the form of supplements, to combat them. You can purchase organic vegetables and meat (free-range, hormone-free, antibiotic-free beef, poultry, and so on) to help eliminate some of these factors, but a good supplement is still necessary to keep the immune system strong.

We recommend the supplements listed below, which can be purchased in a mix and sprinkled on your dog's food. See the resource listing for recommended whole food supplements that contain all of the ingredients below.

- **Probiotics:** You can find these occurring naturally in various foods such as organic yogurt, or in powder form.

- **Digestive enzymes:** If you are feeding a raw diet, the enzymes are naturally occurring in the meat and bone you feed. If you feed a cooked diet or commercial food, you will need to supply your dog with these enzymes in powder or granule form.

- **Vitamin C:** A great, inexpensive source of vitamin C is organic apple cider vinegar. Make sure it has live cultures in it. It can help detoxify your dog's body and even help with body aches and pains.

- **Kelp:** This is a great source for sea minerals and essential omega-3 and omega-6 fatty acids (which help maintain your dog's shiny coat, healthy skin, and overall health). Fish oil is another good source for these essential fatty acids.

- **B-complex:** This supplement is necessary for energy and stamina and to reduce stress in your dog's body. One good way to get a natural source of this is bee pollen.

Again, it is important to do your research and find the best supplements for your dog within your lifestyle and resources. Be sure to read labels, look for certified organic products, and ask other people or your veterinarian what they recommend. Always listen to what your dog is "telling" you through all the outward signs in his body.

Snacks and Treats

There are so many wonderful ways to prepare snacks and treats for your dog. There are lots of home recipes on the market today (in books, magazines, etc.) and many natural treats available for sale online, in pet stores, and by mail order. Do your research to find the best possible source for you and your dog. Look for natural organic treats, and always be sure to read the labels. Just as with regular commercial food, look for treats with the lowest amount of grains or, preferably, no grains at all.

Moving On

Our intention in this chapter was to empower you in making the best choices for feeding your dog. The main principle is that the purer and healthier the food you put into your dog, the healthier your dog will be in the long run. This method of feeding will not prevent your dog from ever getting sick, but it will keep your dog as healthy as possible well into his older years.

We hope this discussion opened up a whole new realm of possibilities for you and your best furry friend in the area of nutrition and health. To help you further in your feeding decisions, please refer to the Resources section at the back of the book. And remember, when in doubt, always seek the advice of your holistic veterinarian.

Labrador Retriever

Chapter Eight

Flea, Tick, and Heartworm Prevention

Fleas, mosquitoes, ticks, and internal parasites are a constant concern to dog caregivers. However, the commonly accepted prevention medicines don't really work as well as the pharmaceutical companies lead us to believe.

Conventional preventive medicines are actually pesticides administered to your dog through prescription pills. A mosquito, flea, or tick will still bite and even infect your dog after he is treated, but the pesticide coursing through your dog's blood kills the

Lurcher

infestation before it becomes disease. Although these pesticides do offer some protection, eventually they can take a toll on your dog's overall health.

The topical remedies sold at pet stores are also pesticides. Even though they may repel fleas, ticks, and mosquitoes, they will eventually be absorbed into your dog's body and could have a negative effect on his health. It is important to remember that any pesticide can cause serious harm to your dog's immune system. We'd prefer not to name any specific brands here, but we will say that there are natural alternatives that provide prevention in the truest sense of the word.

Chemicals such as pesticides may cause considerable harm to your dog's immune system. Remember that a strong, fully supported immune system is the most effective tool in battling pests and disease. You can accomplish this through proper feeding and nutrition and by eliminating any other mitigating factors such as medicines, vaccines, household cleaners, and so forth (please refer to chapters seven and twelve).

Natural repellents in the form of essential oils and herbs offer a much safer approach to warding off pests. In this chapter, we'll offer you some suggestions, but we also want to remind you to do your research and to always be proactive in deciding what will work best for you and your dog.

Essential Oils

As we mentioned earlier, essential oils are complex compounds, which makes them very effective in combating anything that is also natural or virulent in nature, such as mosquitoes, ticks, fleas, and worms. Unlike synthetic medicines, essential oils work with the body rather than against it. Because of this, they can be much more effective at fighting naturally occurring pests.

Know Your Source

One thing to note before beginning to use essential oils is to know your source. According to aromatherapist Kristen Leigh Bell, in her article "Holistic Aromatherapy for the Pampered Pooch," high-quality oils are not typically found in drugstores, grocery stores, or most health food stores. Ms. Bell recommends you obtain essential oils from a small company or individual that sells only aromatherapy-grade, therapeutic oils. Many sources will say their oils are pure, but that may not always be the case. Visit Bell online at www.aromaleigh.com.

Directions for Use

To repel fleas, ticks, or mosquitoes, use essential oils mixed with carrier oil such as organic olive oil in a minimum 50/50 mixture to start. As your dog grows more accustomed to the oils, you can then start to reduce the carrier oil and add more essential oil. However, please note that you can do this with the brand this author uses, but not with most other essential oils. (See Resources, page 168, for a source of these oils.)

Place a couple of drops of the oil mixture in your hand, stir to charge its electrical frequency, and then rub it all over your dog's coat. You can also mix the oils with distilled or filtered water at a minimum 20/80 mixture, and then spray your dog all over lightly. Remember to always keep the oils away from your dog's eyes.

Another option is to purchase shampoos that contain essential oils. Often you can purchase the shampoo from the same supplier you obtain your essential oils from. If you've done your homework and found a very reputable source, ask if they have a shampoo available that not only includes essential oils that are effective at eliminating these pests, but that also doesn't contain any harsh ingredients that may be harmful to your dog's coat, skin, eyes, ears, and other sensitive body parts. Whenever you use essential oils, it's always better to err on the side of caution.

Flea   **Tick**   **Mosquito**

Essential Oil Treatments for Fleas, Ticks, and Mosquitoes

Essential oils are derived from plants, frequently herbs. However, they are different from herbal remedies in that the oils are extracted from various parts of the plant, whereas herbal remedies are made from the entire plant.

Mosquitoes, ticks, and fleas are repelled by a variety of essential oils, but lavender, lemongrass and peppermint are especially effective against most pests that affect your dog's health. The oils will be absorbed into your dog's body through his coat and skin, also providing internal protection. We'll discuss this further in chapter nine.

Essential Oil Treatments for Internal Parasites

Essential oils are also very good at removing internal parasites such as tapeworm or roundworm. Be very careful when administering essential oils internally. I use only one particular brand, which I trust, and wouldn't attempt it with other brands (see Resources, page 168, for more information). As always, please do your research first and err on the side of caution. Diffusing the oils in a nebulizer or diluting them can also help to remove internal parasites. If you are in any doubt, then please do not use essential oils

Dog Knows Best

Keep in mind that your dog has a heightened sense of smell that is far superior to our own. You may want to allow your dog to choose which essential oils he prefers. Amazingly, dogs are very astute at choosing the ones they instinctively know their  individual body needs. Your dog will tell you this by turning away from certain oils, and sniffing or even trying to lick a particular bottle of oil he likes.

internally. Seek the advice of a holistic veterinarian who is familiar with using essential oils before embarking upon this type of treatment.

The following essential oils I use have been proven to be the most effective in eliminating parasites:

Essential Oils Found to Eliminate Parasites

Citronella	Lavender	Peppermint
Clove	Lemon	Rosemary
Fennel	Lemongrass	Rosewood
Hyssop	Mugwort	Tangerine
Idaho Tansy	Nutmeg	Thyme

Diatomaceous Earth and Internal Parasites

Another great internal parasite remover is food-grade diatomaceous earth. Diatomaceous earth is a powder mixture that is mined in the southwestern United States. It is really the skeletal remains of single-cell aquatic plants called diatoms. When diatomaceous earth is milled, the diatoms are covered with microscopic, extremely sharp daggers. When an insect or parasite comes into contact with them, these daggers penetrate the skin of the pests, causing them to dehydrate and eventually die. Insects cannot build up resistance to diatomaceous earth as they do to chemical pesticides, because diatomaceous earth is a natural substance.

You can sprinkle a little on your dog's food and it won't bother him at all, yet it will run those pesky internal parasites right out of town. This is an inexpensive method to ensure that your dog remains parasite-free, plus it also provides an excellent source of trace minerals for your dog. You can also use diatomaceous earth around your yard to control pests and to prevent insect damage to garden plants.

Heartworm

As we stated earlier, traditional prevention medicines do not prevent the mosquito (which transmits heartworm) from biting and infecting your dog; they only kill the infestation that results. In fact, the chemical medicines used in so-called heartworm prevention often compromise your dog's health. Some of the possible side effects are stated right in your veterinarian's medical desk reference. They include liver damage, kidney damage, hair loss, seizures, and more.

The key to heartworm prevention is to prevent the mosquito from not only biting your dog, but from even wanting to bite him in the first place. This starts with providing your dog with the tools he needs for a strong immune system.

Border Collie

Heartworms won't bother with a healthy dog. They want to infest a weakened animal that provides the conditions in which they can grow and thrive. Remember, the nature of a parasite is to consume its host. While it is doing this wonderful chore, it leaves behind by-product toxins, further debilitating the host's health. Once the heartworm parasite reaches and infests the heart, your dog will die of congestive heart failure, if not treated.

Using natural remedies along with the entire protocol we've discussed throughout this book can help your dog ward off heartworm naturally. One option is the homeopathic nosode called Heartworm. We have followed a somewhat long and comprehensive protocol (Heartworm Nosode Support Formula 30C-250 tabs) with our own dogs over an eight-month period to ensure our dogs were protected. This regimen starts as a weekly administering of the Heartworm nosode, which is a homeopathic remedy to strengthen the immune system to resist the actual heartworm infestation. This is followed by a week or two of rest, and then the regimen is started all over again. The last month of this protocol, the dog needs only four homeopathic nosode tablets of 30C strength once a week for a month. Then every year, once a week for one month, he is given the homeopathic nosode of four tablets at 30C strength.

This nosode can be used only in a heartworm-negative dog. That would need to be determined through a blood test performed by your veterinarian prior to using this

Prevent mosquitoes from biting your dog by applying essential oil mixtures of lavender and lemongrass.

method for heartworm prevention.

However, many veterinarians are researching and finding that using nosodes, or prevention medicines, aren't the answer to prevention of heartworm disease in dogs. They are now focusing on improving the natural immunities of dogs through natural feeding, greatly reducing vaccination loads, and boosting the immune system with supplements to keep the dogs they treat free of diseases such as heartworm. Your dog's natural immunities are the best form of defense against invading parasites.

Choosing Heartworm Prevention Medicine

If you live in an area where you know heartworm disease is prevalent, and you choose to put your dog on heartworm prevention medicine, there are some things you can do to lessen the impact on your dog.

Most conventional veterinarians recommend that you keep your dog on this medicine all year, even though the heartworm season occurs only during the warm months when mosquitoes are present. One thing you can do to lessen the load is to only give your dog the medicine during the necessary months of the year. But in warmer climates where mosquitoes live year-round, keeping your dog on this medicine does make sense.

One fact about heartworm medicine most dog caregivers do not know is that it works retroactively. It protects the dog for the previous period of exposure, not against future exposure. The brand we recommend in the resource section actually covers the

If you have young children in the house, it is very important that you keep your dog free of any internal intestinal parasites. If these parasites are inadvertently passed to children, they can cause serious problems. To be prudent, I suggest testing your dog's stool at least twice a year if there are young children in the house.

three months prior to taking the medicine. This information is directly available from the company but not published for public knowledge, yet it is an important advantage to consider when selecting a heartworm medicine.

Give your dog one dose every two months during the warm months, beginning two months after the warm weather begins, and ending when the first cold month hits. By following this protocol, your dog won't be exposed to as many toxins as he would with the conventional dosage, but he will still get the protection he needs.

Please note that there is one downside to the protocol I just described. If your dog does get heartworm disease, the pharmaceutical company would not be responsible for the failure of the product. No preventative treatment is 100 percent effective. This is why the manufacturing companies offer complete reimbursement for any treatment of heartworm disease, should your dog get the disease while using their product as they recommend—with monthly administration. Therefore, if you follow my suggestion and your dog does get heartworm disease, you cannot hold the manufacturer responsible.

Moving On

We hope we have given you enough information to make an informed decision about treating your dog for pests. Remember that prevention is the key, and it can be accomplished with several different natural methods. If you have further questions, please contact a holistic or homeopathic veterinarian in your area, or one who provides telephone consults. In the next chapter, we'll explore several different natural modalities that can help your dog with a variety of ailments.

Chapter Nine

Understanding Natural Remedies: From Herbs to Cod Liver Oil

Nature's plants and creatures provide us with a wide range of natural medicines. Integrate these into the care of your dog as a means of both preventing illness and addressing existing health issues. By being knowledgeable in the use of what nature has provided us, we can help our dogs be well without the overuse of synthetic pharmaceutical products.

Homeopathic Remedies

The underlying belief in homeopathy is that the body has the ability to cure itself; the remedy is only the catalyst. The art of doing homeopathy is to find the remedy that seems to fit the case the best, and select the potency that will cause the most gentle and speedy cure. This requires skill and careful consideration. Many homeopaths have their own phi-

English Springer Spaniel

losophy on which potency to use. Some feel more comfortable with low potencies and some with high potencies. This is all a matter of personal preference.

Homeopathic remedies are made from plant, mineral, or animal products. The process of making a homeopathic remedy is based on a dilution of the initial substance. These remedies are diluted to the point that it *appears* there is nothing in there, but the process of shaking to dilute it stirs up the energetic factor. Once the remedies are diluted to their homeopathic potency, the liquid is poured over sugar pills. The pills then contain the energy of the remedy and will provide what the dog needs.

Sometimes, to make it easier to administer to the dog, veterinarians will suggest mixing the pills in half a glass of water, stirring it around till the pill is dissolved, and then giving a teaspoon of the mixture to the dog. The effect of the remedy is the same whether given in liquid or pill form. The energetic properties of the remedy (in its diluted form) are sensed by the energy in the animal or person's body, and this causes a chain reaction to move the body toward curing itself (assuming that the correct remedy is given).

The different potencies are made according to the number of drops and number of times the remedy is shaken. Remedies range from the X potencies (least potent) to C potencies and then to M potencies (the most potent). The theory is that the lower the potency, the more it causes a reaction in the physical body. The higher the potency, the more it causes a reaction in the mental sphere. However, if it is the correct remedy, almost any potency can cause a curative effect.

In general, if you are using homeopathy yourself, you might want to start with the lower potencies: 6X (known as cell salts or tissue salts) or from 6C to 30C. Lower potencies can be repeated frequently without any side effects. Higher potencies (200C, 1M, etc.) should be repeated less frequently and based on signs that occur after treatment. Usually these signs are best evaluated by a homeopath.

I suggest that you purchase a homeopathic emergency kit, or buy many of the homeopathic remedies listed on the next page, and put together your own kit. Many homeopathic pharmacies sell emergency kits containing thirty to one hundred remedies. Buying these kits is generally very cost-effective.

If you purchase an emergency kit, request the smallest size (#10, pretzel-salt size) pellets. You will get many more of these in each vial, and they tend to stick to the dog's gums/tongue better than the larger (#35, peppercorn-size) pellets. (See Appendix C, page 165 for specific homeopathic remedies for different conditions.)

Recommended Remedies for Homeopathic Emergency Kit

(All in 30C potency except where indicated otherwise.)
Note: ** indicates most important remedies for the emergency kit; others are optional.

Aconitum 30C**

Aconitum 200C

Aconitum 1M**

Allium cepa**

Alumina

Antimonium tartaricum**

Apis**

Arnica**

Arsenicum album**

Belladonna**

Bellis perennis

Bryonia**

Calcarea phosphorica **

Calendula

Cantharis**

Carbo vegetabilis**

Chamomilla**

Cheledonium

China officinalis**

Cocculus**

Coffea cruda

Colocynthis

Drosera

Euphrasia**

Ferrum phosphoricum**

Gelsemium**

Hamamelis

Hepar sulphuris**

Hypericum**

Ignatia**

Ipecac**

Iris versicolor

Kali bichromicum**

Lachesis**

Ledum**

Lycopodium**

Magnesia phosphoricum**

Mercurius vivus**

Nux vomica**

Phosphorous**

Phytolacca

Podophyllum**

Pulsatilla**

Rhus toxicodendron**

Ruta**

Sepia**

Spongia

Staphysagria**

Sulphur**

Symphytum**

Veratrum album**

A Few Basic Guidelines

- For most acute problems, 30C potency is strong enough. A "dose" consists of three pellets (these pellets are the size of peppercorns). They are all basically the same, no matter where you purchase them, because they are all made under strict guidelines and are FDA regulated.

- *Intense, moderate,* and *slow* refer to the intensity of the illness. Acute disease is often very intense, and therefore you can repeat remedies frequently. Remember, intense means life threatening, and that should always be treated on the way to your veterinarian's office.

Illness	Treat with remedy every
Intense	5–90 minutes
Moderate	12–24 hours
Slow	1–4 days

Note: this is based on treatment of 30C potency.

Homeopathy is extremely effective in both acute (sudden onset of illness or symptoms) and chronic (ongoing disease state) disease. Its most dramatic effects and benefits can be seen in the treatment of acute disease. For chronic problems, repetitions are usually less frequent. Please consult with a homeopathic veterinarian for treatment of chronic disease.

- When using a remedy in an emergency or acute condition, if you have given the right remedy, you should see a response within five to ten minutes. This differs from using remedies in chronic, long-standing conditions. Here, most often you will see a gradual improvement of symptoms over several weeks to months. However, you would notice an improvement in energy and well-being within the first week to two weeks. This indicates to most homeopaths that the remedy is acting well, and they will continue to wait for three to four weeks for a follow-up to review the noticed actions of the remedy. All treatment for chronic disease is usually done over a long-range time frame and is usually dependent on the seriousness of the disease being treated and the length of time the dog has been suffering from that disease.

- It is okay to repeat a remedy often until it has a positive effect, which you should be able to tell by how your dog is responding. If you do not see a positive result after three doses of the same remedy, change to the next most likely remedy. Then give that remedy for a total of three doses and so on. The nice thing about homeopathic remedies is that in most instances, even if the body doesn't need that specific remedy (and doesn't resonate with it), the remedy will not cause any unwanted side effect.

- Stop administering the remedy as soon as you see some improvement, even if slight. If your dog appears happier or her symptoms are becoming less intense, this is considered improvement.

Directions for Use

Remedies can be given in several forms: dry pellets or dissolved in water (bottled, distilled, or spring). It is not how much of the mixture is dissolved in water or how many pellets (if given dry), but how many times you give it. This often confuses people. Giving two pellets or four pellets is the same dose as long as you give them all at the same time.

When giving homeopathic remedies, it is best to give them on an empty, clean mouth (separately from food for at least ten minutes). If your dog resists taking the remedy, you can put it in a small amount of baby food, milk, or vanilla ice cream. Remedies can also be placed in your dog's drinking water. After your dog drinks from his bowl, toss the water and fill the bowl with clean water (to avoid repeatedly giving him the remedy.)

Honey Suckle

Aspen

Centaury

Mustard

Sweet Chestnut

Flower Essences

Flower essences can help your dog with a variety of mental and physical disorders, without interfering with any medications he is taking. They are different from vitamins or supplements because rather than work on the physical body of your dog, they work to help support his energy, or life force. In this sense, they are similar to both essential oils and homeopathy. They work in much the same way as homeopathic remedies do, but they come only in liquid form as opposed to tablet or pellet form.

The energy of flower essences comes from the petals and is transferred into water using a special process. The flower petals are placed in a large vat of water and allowed to sit in the sun. The "essence" is transferred to the water. Then the petals are removed and the water itself is used. Essences are preserved in a variety of ways, including with alcohol, vegetable glycerin, white vinegar, and other, more natural substances. Please note that this is a process that can be completed only by those who are certified to do so.

The following chart will help you determine which flower essence to use for your dog's individual situation. Please consult your veterinarian if you are uncertain what to use.

Flower Essence Remedies

Flower Essence	Symptom	Restores
Agrimony	concealed distress	inner peace
Aspen	fear of known	courage
Beech	intolerance	tolerance, flexibility
Centaury	lack of assertiveness	assertiveness, resistance
Cerato	lack of confidence	confidence
Cherry Plum	uncontrollable behavior	control compulsiveness
Chestnut bud	failure to learn	ability to learn from experience
Chicory	possessiveness	normal caring and attention-seeking protectiveness
Clematis	absentmindedness	alertness
Crab apple	uncleanliness, infection, poisoning	cleanliness
Elm	inadequacy	competence
Gorse	hopelessness	endurance
Honeysuckle	homesickness	adjustment to present circumstances
Hornbeam	weakness	vitality
Larch	loss of confidence	confidence
Mimulus	fear	courage
Mustard	depression	serenity
Oak	lack of resilience	resilience
Olive	mental/physical exhaustion	strength
Red chestnut	overprotectivensss	confidence, trust
Rescue Remedy blend	fear, anxiety	calmness (especially while traveling in cars/planes)
Rock rose	terror	courage, calm
Scleranthus	imbalance	balance
Star of Bethlehem	mental and physical shock	calm
Sweet chestnut	distress	endurance
Vervain	impulsiveness	restraint
Vine	dominance, territoriality	positive attitude
Water violet	aloofness	social contact
Willow	maliciousness	good temper

Reprinted, by permission, from *Bach Flower Remedies for Animals* by Helen Graham and Gregory Vlamis, Findhorn Press, 1999.

Directions for Use

Each of the essences listed on the previous pages comes in stock bottles in a concentrated form. Stock bottles and amber-colored dosing bottles can be purchased in health food stores. Dosing bottles will be good for three weeks if stored in a cool place.

Add two drops of the chosen essence or essences (normally, not more than five essences in any one treatment) to 1 ounce (30 milliliters) of natural spring water in a clean dosing bottle. Add one-quarter of a dropper of alcohol (gin or vodka or grain alcohol will do) and top off with distilled water to fill the bottle. From this dosing bottle, give your dog five drops of the mixed essences four times a day. Your dog can take this formula by drinking it or simply absorbing it through his paw pads, ear tips, or skin. Fortunately, most dogs will want to drink a flower essence right down. They seem to instinctively know that the essences will help them get well.

Aromatherapy

Some of you reading this may be thinking, "Aromatherapy for my dog?" Unfortunately, that term has been so loosely tossed about in recent years that it has come to be associated with candles, bath scents, air fresheners, and even incense, but this is far from the original intention of essential oils and aromatherapy. Don't worry, we won't have you lighting candles for your dog as he soaks in a hot bath.

Origins of Aromatherapy

The term *aromatherapy* was coined by Rene-Maurice Gattefosse, the French chemist who wrote the first book on the subject. The original term referred only to therapeutic, superior-quality essential oils, but the term has been subsequently applied loosely to so many things from air freshener to potpourri that the original meaning has become rather distorted.

One day, Dr. Gattefosse burned his arm rather severely in his laboratory, and he quickly stuck his arm into what he thought was a vat of water, when in fact it was a vat of lavender oil. Not only did his pain subside quickly, but his arm healed rapidly and with no scarring. Since then, numerous studies have been conducted on essential oils. As recently as December 2004, scientists in the United Kingdom began researching essential oils to combat the virulent superbug MRSA and found three essential oils that effectively kill this antibiotic-resistant staph infection. (See chapter ten, page 136, for more information on MRSA.)

Therapeutic-Grade Essential Oils

Essential oils are liquid nutrients derived from plants. Think of them as the life force or "blood" of the plants, as their chemical makeup is very similar to human blood and elements of the immune system. Essential oils are alive and electrical in frequency just like your dog's body, which makes them very compatible.

Because they are complex in nature, essential oils can go in and discriminate within the body where they are needed, and take effective action. They work with the body rather than against it. In comparison, antibiotics are synthetic simple compounds that do not discriminate between good and bad bacteria in the body; they just kill everything in their path.

As we've talked about essential oils throughout this book, we've emphasized repeatedly that these oils must be therapeutic-grade oils. Therapeutic-grade essential oils are determined by many factors. Knowing the source of your oils is necessary in order to ensure that you are getting the highest-quality, pure, therapeutic-grade essential oil.

Many in the field of aromatherapy, in particular in the United States and United Kingdom, adhere to the British model of aromatherapy, which has reservations about using any essential oils "neat," or straight on the skin. Industrial-grade essential oils are hastily distilled at high temperature and often have been chemically altered with synthetic solvents, which can actually burn the skin and make using the oils neat unsafe. Since this market is basically unregulated, these solvents are added to bring a greater yield to the oils for more profit. These industrial-grade oils are really only good for perfume, and not for healing, as their chemical compounds have been rendered basically useless during processing.

Essential oils are the "plasma" part of the plant and are extracted from the seeds, leaves, bark, roots, and flowers of various plants.

In this book, however, we adhere strictly to the French and German models of aromatherapy, which indicate use of essential oils neat and/or diffused. The essential oils we use exclusively are listed in the resource section. *These are the only essential oils we use, suggest, or refer to throughout this book,* and we are confident in using them in the manner stated herein. We do not suggest using any other brands of oils in the manner referred to in this book.

To be able to determine whether something is therapeutic grade, you must understand how the oils are grown and produced. The following guidelines will help you determine if your oils are therapeutic grade:

1. Make sure your oils are grown free of pesticides, chemicals, and herbicides. Any of these substances can create a chemical change in the oils, which will then allow toxic compounds to form in the oil.

2. Only organic fertilizers should be applied. The richest, finest oils are grown in the richest, nutrient-dense soils.

3. True therapeutic-grade oils will be very slowly distilled at the lowest possible temperature in stainless steel to ensure that all of the healing, aromatic compounds within the plant remain intact. The distillation process is critical.

4. Use price as a clue. Therapeutic-grade oils are often significantly higher in price than industrial grade oils.

What can be done using essential oils is as vast as the oils themselves. These little therapeutic agents can go into the body and repair everything right down to the DNA. In fact, these oils can clean out and oxygenate your dog's blood all at once, making them a powerful weapon to add to your natural care defense and prevention team. Please refer to our chart for some of the oils and their uses. Do your aromatherapy homework, and you may even discover new ways for using essential oils to care for your dog.

For any problems not addressed in this chart, consult a holistic veterinarian. Remember to always consult your holistic veterinarian first for any serious problems, illness, disease, or injuries. Take your dog in for a full exam; do not attempt to self-diagnose or embark upon treatment without a diagnosis. Be sure to take into consideration all the factors discussed in the previous chapters, and do not use any essential oil without (1) ascertaining if it is therapeutic grade and (2) consulting your veterinarian, especially for the more serious problems with your dog.

Note: Essential oils have not been evaluated by the Food and Drug Administration.

Essential Oils for Aromatherapy

Problem	Oils
Arthritis	Wintergreen, vetiver, helichrysum, lemongrass
Allergies	Lavender, ledum, German chamomile, Roman chamomile
Parasites	Citronella, eucalyptus globulus
Inflammation	Pine, wintergreen
Sprains	Lemongrass, lavender
Mites	Peppermint
Respiratory	Pine, myrtle, Eucalyptus radiata
Trauma	Lavender, valerian, chamomile, melissa, rosewood
Irritable bowel syndrome	Peppermint, fennel, tarragon
Lyme disease	Thyme, oregano, clove, melissa
Obesity	Peppermint, ylang ylang

How to Apply Essential Oils

1. Direct inhalation. Put a drop or two in your hands, and allow your dog to sniff them. Your dog will show you if he wants to inhale by crinkling his nose when you open a bottle. Dogs are very specific in their body language when they like or dislike something, so pay attention to how your dog reacts to any essential oil you decide to try with him or her.

2. Diffuse essential oils in a cold-air diffuser. This is the simplest way to get the oils into the air for inhaling. These diffusers can be purchased from different suppliers such as www.abundanthealth4u.com and come in a variety of styles. Our preference is a nebulizer. Cold-air diffusers use air at room temperature to blow the essential oil up against the glass nebulizer. This causes the oils to break up into a micromist that permeates the air and can cover hundreds of square feet very quickly. These diffusers can get the essential oils into the air of your home fast and efficiently. In our opinion, this may be better than using an air filter and is certainly less expensive, plus it improves the quality of air within the home.

3. Direct application. If you decide to apply the essential oils directly to your dog's skin, do so initially using a mixing oil such as pure, organic olive oil in a 50/50 mixture, and apply the oil mixture to the pads of your dog's feet. Because the dog

may lick her paws, the essential oils you use must be safe for consumption. Therefore, for this type of application, we advise you to use only the essential oils suggested on page 116.

Understand that while herbs are a great addition to caring for your dog, they are best used in conjunction with natural feeding and supplementation, to provide your dog with the highest-quality overall support and care.

Herbs

Plants are nature's medicine cabinet, and as you've seen throughout this chapter, the entire plant can be used. From the flower petals for essences to the plant's "blood" or life force for essential oils to the dried plant for herbs, plants are a great source of healing for our dogs. The key is to use herbs and herbal products that are made from only certified organic plants, meaning those that were grown pesticide-free and herbicide-free and in mineral-rich soils. All of these factors weigh in to how good these plant sources will be for healing in your dog.

While traditional medicines or pharmaceuticals isolate single active ingredients from a plant or create synthetic look-alikes, herbal remedies focus on using the whole plant or parts of the whole plant in order to create a naturally occurring complex compound. Similar to homeopathy and flower essences, traditional herbalism depends upon each dog's unique personality and current medical condition, whereas modern herbalism places its primary focus or treatment upon the actual herb rather than your dog. Because of this difference, uses and treatments can be quite different between the two forms of herbalism.

Herbs to Avoid

Comfrey

Pennyroyal

Hops

Tea tree

Traveling with Your Dog

Many of us travel with our dogs. It's always such a good feeling knowing they can come along and not be left home alone. However, even though our dogs may be used to traveling a short distance in the car, long distances can give them upset stomachs or dizziness. Traveling by plane can be an altogether harrowing and stressful situation for even the most seasoned traveling dog. Fortunately, there are some natural remedies to help make this trip more pleasant for both you and your dog.

Therapeutic-grade essential oils help to calm and settle your dog during extended travel because they work not only on the physical part of your dog, but also on his emotions—his mind and spirit. Ginger is one of the first oils that comes to mind for motion sickness; it has anti-inflammatory properties as well as digestive properties. This fragrant oil can stimulate gentleness within your dog and help stimulate physical energy along with courage—a great combination for an anxiety-ridden nauseous dog. Ginger is considered a warm oil, meaning it can feel warm or sometimes even hot on the skin, especially if it is not diluted.

Peppermint is another great essential oil, and is considered a hot oil. It can initially feel mentholated to the skin, but when inhaled, it is refreshing and cool like a breath mint. It is a very versatile oil, in that it can calm a nervous stomach and is also antiparasitic. This should be diluted with mixing oil before applying.

Rescue Remedy, which is a combination of five flower essences, can be very helpful when traveling with your dog if he gets nervous. It is especially good for any situation where your dog experiences anxiety (car rides, visits to the veterinarian's office, company coming over to the house, thunderstorms, etc.). Other essential oils and flower essences specifically beneficial during travel are listed in the chart below.

Flower Essence	What It Is Used For	Essential Oil	What It Is Used For
Cerato	Lack of confidence	Ginger, patchouli, peppermint	Nausea
Rescue Remedy	Fear, anxiety		
Larch	Loss of confidence	Ginger, lavender, patchouli, peppermint, spearmint	Motion sickness
Mimulus	Fear		
Rock rose	Terror	German chamomile, Roman chamomile, lavender, peppermint, and valerian	Nervous anxiety
Sweet chestnut	Distress		

Caution: Never wash essential oils out with water as that can make the eyes burn. Use a mixing oil to dilute and relieve burning sensation.

Herbal Remedies

Herb	What It Is Used For
Astragalus	Immune booster
Boswellia	Arthritis
Burdock	Allergies
Chamomile	Wounds (topical)
Cranberry	Urinary tract infections
Echinacea	Immune booster, respiratory infections
Garlic	Immune booster, colds, bacterial infections, parasites
Ginger	Motion sickness, nausea, dizziness, digestion problems
Goldenseal	Infections
Hawthorn	Heart trouble, circulation
Lavender	Nervous disorders, pain
Milk thistle	Liver disorders
Nettle	Allergies
Peppermint	Nausea, indigestion

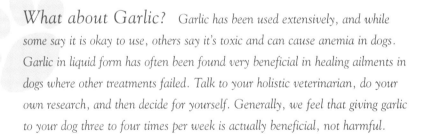

What about Garlic? *Garlic has been used extensively, and while some say it is okay to use, others say it's toxic and can cause anemia in dogs. Garlic in liquid form has often been found very beneficial in healing ailments in dogs where other treatments failed. Talk to your holistic veterinarian, do your own research, and then decide for yourself. Generally, we feel that giving garlic to your dog three to four times per week is actually beneficial, not harmful.*

Directions for Use

Because different suppliers supply different directions for using their specific herbs, and amounts are very specific to dog sizes, directions can't be clearly defined as with flower essences or essential oils. Please use herbs under the direction of an herbalist or veterinarian versed in this area.

Fish Oil

Our grandparents and their parents knew all about taking their daily dose of cod-liver oil. While the sound of it may not be very appealing, the essential fatty acids (EFAs) found in it are critical to a dog's health.

We often hear EFAs referred to as omega-3s and omega-6s. These substances serve a number of vital functions in our dog's body. From the metabolism of triglycerides and cholesterol to brain, nerve, and adrenal function, EFAs are the key factors. This means that they are responsible for stimulating and increasing metabolic rate, along with being responsible for helping breathing, and energy.

Fish is the best way to provide your dog with these valuable EFAs. However, the problem with fish is its high content of mercury and other heavy metals. Make sure your dog is getting fish that is not farmed but wild, from pristine, untainted waters. By doing this, you'll ensure that your dog is getting his omega-3s and omega-6s in the correct balance.

If you cannot find wild fish, fish oil and cod-liver oil are the best sources for omega-3s. Evening primrose oil, borage oil, and black currant oil are your dog's best sources for omega-6s and can be purchased from any health food store. To provide all the necessary EFAs, consider giving your dog pure, organic cold-pressed virgin coconut oil. This type of coconut oil is not only EFA rich, but it also has trace minerals and necessary enzymes, making it a great food source. (See Resources, page 168.)

Directions for Use

In lieu of good food sources, supplements must be used. Dosage guidelines follow:

For small dogs, give one-eighth the dose of the human recommendation.

For medium dogs, give one-fourth the dose of the human recommendation.

For large dogs, give one-half to a full dose of the human recommendation.

Moving On

As you've seen in this chapter, nature provides us with a plethora of safe, effective remedies for treating our dogs. In the next chapter, we'll discuss more traditional methods of caring for your dog and some of the potential pitfalls associated with those methods.

Chapter Ten

Traditional Veterinary Care: From Medicine to Surgery

Throughout this book we've discussed all the ways to care for your dog. From building up his immune system with natural feeding and supplementation to avoiding overvaccination to using natural modalities and homeopathic preparations, we've covered the gamut to help you proactively care for your dog. Now, let's look at what a traditional vet does to combat illness or disease in your dog.

As a dog caregiver, you will often be responsible for administering medicine. Most dogs resist this, and it can be a challenge. However, once you find a routine that works, your dog will get used to it, and it should become easier. Hiding a pill in peanut butter, for example, is a very effective approach.

Cocker Spaniel

Commonly Prescribed Medications

Most conventional veterinarians give every dog across the board the same treatment for the same problem. In many cases, the treatment will consist of antibiotics and/or steroids. These are the commonly accepted treatments in the conventional realm of medicine. The reason they are prescribed is because they usually work quickly to resolve the apparent problem, and it appears to the average dog caregiver that the problem has been cured.

On the other hand, the holistic veterinarian usually looks at these treatments as suppressive, meaning that they suppress the immune system from reacting to the initial cause of the problem. Therefore, the dog seems better in the short term, but on an overall, long-term basis, he is really getting worse. What you may notice is that the initial problem seems to recur, sometimes chronically. In that case, more antibiotics are again prescribed—often in higher doses, which are needed to effectively resolve the same problem a second (or third, or more) time. Or, steroids may be needed for a longer and longer period of time to solve the problem each time it resurfaces. In fact, some dogs end up taking steroids for their entire lives.

If the dog is unable to expel the toxins (disease) through discharge (because this natural function is suppressed by the antibiotic or steroid), eventually the internal organs will get overtaxed from their attempt to get rid of these toxins and will start to break down. Homeopaths see this as a natural progression after a dog has experienced a lot of suppression through antibiotics and steroids. The disease goes "deeper" into the dog. This deeper disease is often much more difficult to cure because it is "man-made" or "chemically made" (all those antibiotics and steroids repeated over time). We often see this in cases of dogs with bad skin disease that has been treated repeatedly with antibiotics and steroids, resulting a few years later in liver or kidney disease.

However, there are times when antibiotics and steroids may be needed and are, indeed, lifesaving. After you and your veterinarian discuss their use and you understand the reasons, we do suggest you follow those treatments. Depending on the severity of the illness, you can also request a second opinion or consult with a holistic veterinarian to see what other course of treatment you can engage in simultaneously or after the conventional treatment.

Side Effects of Antibiotics

Antibiotics have been so overused that new, extremely virulent superbugs such as MRSA are emerging and evolving. The problem does not lie with the medical community alone. Our society wants the quick fix. We don't want to see our dogs suffering. Remember, antibiotics are not really a quick fix; rather they can be a major contributor to the decline of your dog's health, especially when they are used over and over again.

Antibiotics, by their very nature, are bacteria-killing agents. Unfortunately, antibiotics do not discern between the bad or the much-needed good bacteria. Your dog needs to have about 80 percent good bacteria in his intestinal tract and approximately 20 percent bad bacteria. When you give him antibiotics, the balance is reversed. In fact, the antibiotics may seemingly help your dog get over whatever ailment he is suffering from, only to suffer from another malady later on. When the normal eco-balance in your dog's body is disrupted due to a nondiscriminating factor such as antibiotics, your dog's body will subsequently be imbalanced. Even if you do all the things we've suggested in this book, it can still take your dog's intestinal tract up to one year to be recolonized by bacteria in the proper balance after taking antibiotics.

Side Effects of Steroids

While steroids may provide instant relief and appear to be curative, they can, in fact, do much damage to your dog's body. The veterinary profession has, in a sense, thrown up its hands and given in to client demands by giving steroids and antibiotics immediately rather than as a last resort. Normally steroids are the standard drug of choice for allergies, arthritis, pain, and so on. While we may want to blame a multitude of sources for this blatant overuse of this drug, we are ultimately the responsible party.

Steroids are harmful because they imitate the function of the adrenal glands. Adrenal glands are responsible for regulating your dog's metabolism. The steroid itself does nothing to cure your dog of anything, but rather suppresses the normal body response, such as in the case of allergies. An allergic reaction is a response to something that the body should not react to. Steroids suppress an allergic reaction but do

Akita

not get at the root of the problem that is causing the allergy in the first place. While your dog may seem better initially, using steroids on a regular basis can ultimately lead to other, more serious problems (such as diabetes, muscle wasting, allow infections to get worse by suppressing the immune system, etc.). Most dogs on steroids will have an increase in their eating and drinking, need to urinate more, and possibly pant excessively.

Alternatives to Antibiotics and Steroids

Of course, finding the actual cause of the illness and building up your dog's immune system is a better approach. Many holistic veterinarians report outstanding results treating the common diseases with alternative and complementary approaches instead of antibiotics and steroids.

If you only take one piece of advice from this book, we hope you get the message that you have many options for treatment when your dog gets ill. No matter how negative the prognosis given by your conventional veterinarian, at least make one or two telephone calls to a holistic veterinarian to get his or her view of what might be possible for your dog. In my experience, when a conventional vet gives a dire prognosis, 75 percent of the time homeopathy or some other holistic modality has made a significant improvement in a dog's health. And time and time again it has extended the life of the dog or cured the problem originally thought to be hopeless.

Please see Appendix C, page 165, for specific holistic remedies that can be used in place of traditional medicines for numerous different conditions.

Nonsteroidal Anti-inflammatory Drugs

Often dogs with arthritis are prescribed some nonsteroidal anti-inflammatory drugs. Rimadyl and Metacam are two of these commonly prescribed drugs. Both are like very strong aspirin. Never give them at the same time as you are giving regular aspirin to your dog.

Recently these types of drugs given to human beings have been recalled because of serious side effects such as heart disease. Our dogs do not necessarily get heart-related symptoms. Instead, these drugs can cause serious liver disease and, in some cases, death. If your dog is ever put on these drugs, your veterinarian should first test your dog's blood chemistry to be assured that he does not already have any problems with his liver. Once you administer these drugs, it is very important to monitor your dog's liver enzymes regularly. These drugs should be used at the lowest possible dose to prevent painful movement.

Another side effect of these drugs is that they may cause internal bleeding or ulcers. If you notice any signs of blood in your dog's stool, urine, vomit, etc.), immediately stop giving these drugs and speak with your veterinarian.

Surgery

Many conditions require conventional treatment in the form of surgery, and it is never to be taken lightly. Most dogs and their caregivers first experience this around six months of age, when the dog is neutered or spayed. Even though this is a normal procedure, most caregivers are reluctant and fearful of putting their dog under anesthesia.

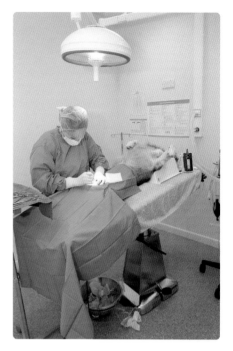

There are many instances where surgery can be lifesaving or required to correct a serious problem. Surgery is often necessary to:

- Fix broken bones

- Correct disc disease

- Remove life-threatening tumors

- Remove an eyelid growth that is rubbing against a dog's eye and causing the eye to be irritated or ulcerated

- Remove a foreign object that seemed simple to swallow but then blocked the dog's intestinal track

- Repair a diaphragmatic rupture (organs from the abdominal cavity push through the diaphragm and into the chest cavity. This can be a life-threatening situation or something a veterinarian may notice on X-ray by accident. Some dogs live with this condition without showing any signs of distress for years.)

- Explore, flush, and install a drain in a dog-bite wound (A drain is a rubber tube or sterile cotton string that is put into a pocket of skin that is torn away from the body due to a dog bite or abscess. It allows the body to drain off whatever substance is building up in that pocket and remove it from the body.)

Whenever these instances occur, you need to make sure your dog is in the best hands for the procedure. Ask your veterinarian if she specializes in the specific procedure, and how many of these procedures she does a week, a month, or a year. The credentials of the doctor are also important. How long has he or she been practicing? If your veterinarian doesn't have as much experience as you'd like, seek out another vet with the experience you are comfortable with. You may need to seek out a specialist, especially for any spinal surgery or orthopedic surgery.

If you have time, always try to get a second opinion from a specialist before submitting your dog to surgery with a general veterinary practitioner. You might also contact a holistic veterinarian. Any reputable veterinarian will be happy to share your dog's records at your request. In some cases, there may be a holistic or homeopathic or alternative treatment to try before going to surgery. Of course, this is always based on the severity of the dog's condition, but if you are not sure how to proceed, take the time to call other people and discuss it with them.

Presurgery

With every surgery there is always a risk when the dog is under anesthesia. These days, most veterinary practices use the latest in anesthesia during surgery, but there is no harm in asking about their procedures and what type of anesthesia is used. Also inquire about the pain-control regimen the doctor uses. Many veterinarians use pain medication before, during, and after surgery to alleviate traumatic pain and ensure a smoother recovery for the patient.

If the dog is over five years old, a veterinarian usually requires that full blood work be completed so that he can adjust the anesthesia, time on the operating table, and other considerations before starting the surgery. For older dogs, some veterinarians also

Boston Terrier

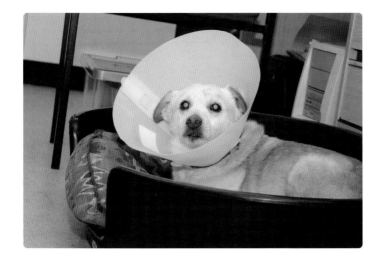

An Elizabethan collar is often used to keep a dog from licking, chewing, or removing sutures or otherwise bothering a wound that needs to heal. This collar is designed so that the dog's mouth cannot reach beyond the collar to make contact with its body.

require a chest X-ray, an ECG, or other presurgical tests. Even for young puppies, many veterinarians are now requiring some of these diagnostic tests. In the case of young, healthy dogs, these tests usually come back negative. However, for the few dogs in which some sign of disease or problem is detected before going to surgery, these diagnostic tests are very important.

If your veterinarian requires any presurgical testing, feel free to ask him the purpose of each test, and evaluate the need for these tests according to the procedures being performed. Just think of the extent of the medical tests done on people prior to surgery. The medical profession wants to know everything it can ahead of time. This is practicing good medicine.

You'll also want to inquire about aftercare, especially if your dog will be required to stay overnight. Find out if there is twenty-four-hour care, or if the staff and doctors leave at a certain time and the dog will be alone until the next morning. Ask if your dog will require any treatment overnight, such as intravenous fluids or medicines, and who will administer these treatments. If it is a serious condition, you'll want to find a facility that offers twenty-four-hour care. For spays and neuters, the dogs just need to be quiet and rest all night, so they will not usually require any overnight treatment. However, whenever possible, it is always best to have twenty-four-hour coverage. Anything can happen.

Postsurgery

Once your dog comes home, there are homeopathic remedies I always prescribe to speed healing, prevent or resolve bruising, reduce pain, and take away the traumatic experience of being separated from his caregiver. Please refer to chapter eleven for more information about remedies for emergency conditions.

By keeping your dog healthy through proper feeding and nutrition, you'll be able to avoid, as much as possible, things such as dental cleanings and routine surgery your dog would need to undergo over time. Remember, prevention is key.

How to Ease the Pain After Surgery

Type of Surgery	Homeopathic Remedy	Frequency	Reason
Dental cleanings	Arnica montana	30C (3 pellets) three times a day for one to three days	To alleviate pain and the effects of trauma
Teeth extraction	Arnica montana and Hypericum perforatum	Hypericum perforatum 30C (3 pellets) once a day, Arnica montana 30C (3 pellets) twice a day for three days, or until the dog seems back to himself and eating well	To alleviate pain and the effects of trauma (Hypericum is specifically for pain to the nerves.)
General surgery	Arnica montana, Staphysagria, Calendula	Arnica montana 30C (3 pellets) in the morning, for three to seven days Staphysagria 30C (3 pellets) in the afternoon, for three to seven days Calendula 30C (3 pellets) in the evening, for three to seven days	To alleviate pain, especially that from the knife wound, and to speed healing
Abdominal surgery or spay	Arnica montana, Staphysagria, Calendula	Arnica montana 30C (3 pellets) in the morning, for three to seven days Staphysagria 30C (3 pellets) in the afternoon, for three to seven days, or replace with Bellis perennis 30C (3 pellets) after the first day Calendula 30C (3 pellets) in the evening, for three to seven days.	To alleviate pain, especially from the knife wound, and to speed healing. (Bellis perennis is especially effective on the internal organs.)

Chapter Eleven

Be Your Dog's Medical Advocate

As one of the millions of loving dog caregivers, you will always be alert to changes in your dog's normal behavior. However, many of us have very busy lives, and while we may observe a change in our dog or see something unusual, we may decide to wait a few days before doing anything about it. By the time a few days have passed, our dog may have gotten a lot worse. Then we panic. We rarely hear a dog caregiver say they are sorry they took their dog to the vet. But we have often heard someone say they wish they hadn't waited so long.

Please pay attention to those early warning signs and take action as soon as you notice the changed behavior. At the early stages of a problem, you can utilize many of the alternative treatments suggested in this book. If you have read all the chapters leading up to this one, you are well equipped to handle most emergencies and to treat the early signs of problems. You should also know by now that there are some occasions when taking your dog immediately to the veterinarian while administering alternative treatments is the best, safest approach.

In this chapter we will give you some tips for how to make the best possible decisions for your dog's health when unfortunate issues arise, and advise you of certain substances that can be poisonous to your furry friend. Don't forget that as a dog caregiver, you, and only you, are responsible for managing his health.

Don't Blame Yourself

Dogs get unexpectedly sick just as humans do. When these circumstances arise, it is important that you discuss all the different aspects of your dog's life with his veterinarian and try to find the cause. Remember that it is always okay to question things and to ask for a more in-depth explanation or alternative treatments.

One question most people ask when their dogs get sick is "Why did this happen?" Unfortunately, there are so many things in life that we find out about only when they actually become a problem. What seems to be behind this question is the caregiver's fear that perhaps he did something wrong that caused the problem, or didn't do something that could have prevented the problem. But the best answer to this difficult question is that the problem happened because it happened.

When people get sick, we can look to genetics, personal habits, longtime stress, or something outside of a person that contributes to her illness. With animals, this is very difficult to determine. Often we don't know their genetics, and we cannot interpret what might be stressful for them. Rather than feeling guilty when your dog gets ill, we suggest you put all that love into researching what can be done for your dog's problem.

If a conventional veterinarian tells you there is nothing more he can do for your dog, you may, understandably, feel devastated. However, we recommend you immediately research and seek out an alternative veterinarian. Get a second and third opinion. At least one-third of my practice is filled with clients who have heard that statement and didn't give up. There is definitely a time to accept the inevitable, but don't do it so easily, no matter what diagnosis you get for your dog.

There are alternative or complementary treatments that can be helpful and even curative. There are many options out there for you and your dog. Ask friends about their experiences, talk to people at holistic pet stores, search the Internet, go to your local bookstore—just don't give up. Call an animal communicator to see if she can give you more information. What have you got to lose? Your dog may be the initiator of your finding a whole new holistic health path for the both of you. Don't give up until you have exhausted all options.

When patients respond so positively to homeopathy, it seems like magic. However, it's not magic. It's time tested and honored medical treatment. Homeopathic treatment principles and remedies are over 200 years old. There is a lot of research to prove homeopathic medicine works. Open your mind and your heart to what is out there.

Success Story

Glen brought his eighteen-year-old, fifteen-pound (6.8-kg) male poodle to see me several years ago. Benny had been diagnosed with congestive heart failure two years earlier and was taking a lot of conventional medication for his condition. However, he was coughing and generally not doing well.

Glen was hoping that homeopathy could help him. Although Benny was old, he had a lot of spirit and Glen thought he had a lot of life left in him. We started homeopathic treatment of a low daily dose of Phosphorous LM1. I chose this remedy based on Benny's very friendly and happy personality, and the signs of his illness.

This remedy has an affinity for the respiratory tract. In addition, I put Benny on Hawthorne (10 drops a day added to his drinking water). Hawthorne is a tincture that nourishes and supports the heart. I would see Glen and Benny every three months to refill his remedy and monitor his condition. It was such a joy to see him doing so well for so long. Benny stayed on that remedy for a least one year and then we graduated to Phosphorous LM2.

Benny lived a happy, joyful, and fairly active life, to the ripe old age of twenty-one.

Typical Case

Buddy, a ten-year-old, sixty-five-pound (29.5-kg) mixed breed dog was brought to me in September 2002 by his caregiver, Carol. He was in great distress and had difficulty walking. Buddy had been diagnosed as having a large tumor at the end of his spine. It was in an area that could not be biopsied, so we never were able to get an accurate diagnosis. Carol's veterinary oncologist had told her that unless Buddy had chemotherapy and/or radiation within a month, he would not be able to walk anymore and would have to be euthanized.

Carol did not want to do chemotherapy or radiation, but she did not want to give up on Buddy just yet. She asked me if there was anything I could do. As soon as he started homeopathic treatment, Buddy seemed to be in less pain. I started Buddy on the homeopathic remedy Nitric acid 200C. One month later, Carol reported that Buddy's personality had returned to normal and that Buddy did not seem to have any more pain. He was playful, happy, eating, and walking well.

One month later, he was not doing well again. There seemed to be more growths on his paw and the side of his body, and he had diarrhea from eating garbage. Nux vomica 30C was given and it resolved his acute diarrhea. Fortunately, his diagnostic procedures determined that the growths were benign.

I then treated him with Lyssin 200C to counteract the effects of the rabies vaccine administered by his conventional vet. Buddy was fine until seven months later, when he was diagnosed with thyroid cancer. The veterinarian successfully removed this cancer, and I gave Buddy a dose of Spongia 200C to help him recover.

One month later, because of changes in Buddy's personality, I gave him Lycopodium 200C. After that remedy, he seemed back to his good old self and very energetic and happy. But approximately one year later, Buddy started to show symptoms of being ill again, and I repeated the Lycopodium 200C treatment.

Buddy became anemic. He received conventional treatment for this condition, and I also put him on the tissue salt Ferrum phosphoricum 6x (daily). This is a very low-dose homeopathic remedy that is similar to an iron supplement but encourages the body to stabilize itself and reverse the anemia.

Buddy's case is a good example of the typical case that homeopaths see. The remedy needed to keep changing because the picture the animal presented kept changing. That is why it is important for an caregiver to work with a trained homeopathic veterinarian when dealing with this type of serious disease.

Happy Ending

Sammy was a ten-year-old, eighty-seven-pound (39.5-kg), happy yellow Labrador Retriever when Barbara brought him to see me. The main problem was that Sammy needed to go out to urinate at least four to six times a day. He was also drinking water constantly. When he was a young dog, he had been diagnosed with a low specific gravity (1.007) from birth. This means his kidneys did not function well and were not uptaking urine from his system as they should have.

Barbara was told that there was no conventional treatment for him, so she and Sammy were just living with the problem. Since Barbara and Sammy lived in an apartment in New York City, this was very inconvenient.

Barbara brought Sammy to me without much hope for improvement. After our first meeting, I started Sammy on a homeopathic treatment of Rhus toxicodendron (30C) because he was slightly arthritic and had many ritualistic behaviors such as having to cross the street at the same place and on a diagonal every time. I also prescribed some supplements—¼ teaspoon (1 g) of baking soda in his food, and a tea made from dandelion, alfalfa, and nettles, taken three times a day to flush and purify the kidneys. He also was given ¼ teaspoon (1 g) ghee butter to nourish his kidneys.

His homeopathic treatments changed over time, and his personality traits seemed to change as well. The remedy that seemed to be most effective with him was Lycopodium. He would seem calmer and have less urgency to urinate after taking it. After several months of treatment, Sammy's specific gravity moved from a low 1.007 to a normal 1.017 (normal range is 1.015–1.040). This allowed him to sleep through the night most nights and go on three to four walks a day instead of six or more. Over the next three years, we treated him for many other problems as they came up, such as arthritis and fearfulness. Each time he improved both physically and emotionally. At age thirteen he lost his last fight, due to cancer. However, Barbara was grateful that he lived a longer, happier, and healthier life with homeopathy.

When Is It Time to Let Go?

There is no right answer here. It is very personal. We would never dictate this answer. You are the one who has to live with your choice in the matter. Each person involved needs to be honest about his or her emotional and financial limits. You will know when it's time.

I often tell dog caregivers, "As long as your dog is eating and drinking and able to get around and not in pain, then whatever you can do to extend her life is fine. When these things start to change, then it's time to consider relieving the dog's suffering." Many caregivers choose to let their dogs go naturally, and others want the veterinarian to assist in this process. Although we don't like to think about this time in our dog's life, it is helpful to consider these questions:

- What are your limits?

- Would you decide to euthanize your dog if you thought it was his time to go, or to end his suffering?

- Would you want someone to come to the house, or would you want to take him to your local vet?

Find out what is involved with this process, and allow your trusted veterinarian to help you make this decision. He or she knows you and your dog very well and can assist you at this difficult time.

Poisonous Substances to Avoid

Lurcher

Dogs are like children—they are curious, and you need to keep harmful substances out of their reach. As your dog's medical mentor, you need to make sure you keep the following things in a safe place where your clever pal can't access them.

- Most human medicines—including those for heart disease, high blood pressure, and hyperthyroid; antidepressants; aspirin; and so on.

- All narcotics—including marijuana, hashish, and hallucinogens. If your dog ingests a narcotic, he may need in-patient medical treatment until fully recovered.

- Products containing organophosphates (OP), carbamate, and chlorinated hydrocarbon (CIHC)—such as flea- and tick-repelling collars. These collars have poisonous substances that are supposed to be on the dog's skin and not ingested. Ingesting them can cause neurological signs that may require in-patient care, depending on the severity of the condition.

- Bleach can be very harmful if swallowed or even licked. It can burn your dog's esophagus and stomach lining as it gets swallowed. Never induce vomiting in this instance. Give your dog lots of water and milk to help dilute the bleach.

- Chocolate and caffeine—depending on the amount ingested. If your dog consumes either of these, it is okay to induce vomiting, but your dog may also need medical treatment. The ingredients in chocolate and coffee products that make them so dangerous for dogs are methylxanthine alkaloids (compounds that are part of the natural molecular makeup of these products), particularly theobromine and caffeine. Unlike humans, dogs do not possess the enzyme necessary to break down theobromine. Because of this, theobromine will continue to accumulate in your dog's body over time if he is allowed to continue to consume chocolate. While he may

Keep activated charcoal (to absorb poisonous substances if ingested) and ipecac (to induce vomiting) in your medicine cabinet just in case you ever need them. Ask your veterinarian to advise you of the appropriate amount (determined by the size of your dog) of each of these to give so you are prepared ahead of time. Write this information on the bottles so you always have it handy..

not get sick the first time he eats it (however, hyperactivity will probably be pretty evident due to the sugar and caffeine), eventually your dog will become toxic with chocolate and could ultimately die from this toxicity. Err on the side of caution and avoid allowing your dog to have chocolate altogether.

Some over-the-counter drugs also have these ingredients, so be very careful with these substances around your dog. Vomiting and/or diarrhea will usually happen within two to four hours after eating the chocolate or coffee product. Your dog will also show signs of extreme nervousness and maybe even have tremors and seizures or excessive urinating. Prognosis is good if you catch the problem within two to four hours of your dog's ingesting the substance. Don't induce vomiting if your dog is having a seizure; just get him to a veterinarian quickly. However, you should get your dog to a veterinarian even if he has vomited up the substance. Be safe rather than sorry.

- Onions and garlic—depending on the amount eaten, can cause anemia. Your dog may need a blood transfusion and in-patient care. Garlic can be given cautiously whole, or as liquid three to four times a week.

- Zinc—found in nuts, bolts, and pennies minted after 1983. This can cause anemia if the substances are ingested. Lead is also found in some coins, old paints, and toys. If your dog swallows things such as coins or toys, he may need surgery to remove the foreign body, and hospitalization for in-patient care.

- Rat poison can be very dangerous even in small doses. If you see your dog ingest rat poison, induce vomiting and give her activated charcoal within fifteen minutes; this will help to minimize the effect. Then take her immediately to the veterinarian for observation.

  If you don't see your dog ingest the poison, be advised that she may look normal for twenty-four to seventy-two hours before showing signs of poisoning (bleeding from anywhere: nose, rectum, mouth/gums, urinary tract, etc.). By the time you see these signs, it may be too late to save your dog. Seek immediate care if you think she has eaten rat poison, and whenever possible, bring the name of the rat poison with you to your veterinarian.

If you think your pet has ingested ANY AMOUNT of a toxic substance, it is crucial that you take immediate action. Always have the number of the nearest animal hospital or a local animal poison hotline posted somewhere obvious in your house. The veterinarian will tell you if what your dog ate was poisonous or could cause a problem, and will advise you of what treatment is needed (or if you need to seek immediate medical attention). If the substance was not dangerous to your dog, this call will relieve your concern. It is always better to err on the side of being overly safe rather than sorry.

Chapter Twelve

Environmental Toxins and Natural Solutions

Throughout this book we've discussed the various things that contribute to poor or ill health in our dogs. From commercially processed foods to overvaccination, many "normal" practices wreck havoc on our dogs' already overtaxed immune systems. In this chapter, we'll discuss how your dog's environment can have a negative effect on his health.

Outdoor Chemicals

Hopefully your dog spends a lot of time outside, playing, sunbathing, and relaxing. As this is often the case, it is important to realize that the chemical fertilizers, pesticides, and herbicides used on yards can have negative effects on not only the soil and wildlife, but on your dog's health, too. All of these products can enter your dog's body through his feet and skin and will have long-lasting effects on his overall health. Symptoms of chemical reactions can mask themselves as allergies, seizures, or rashes and can ultimately result in some form of cancer if your dog is continually exposed to these products in your yard. By changing to natural, organic products, you are allowing your dog and your environment to thrive naturally.

The labels on many outdoor chemical products list warnings such as "fatal or dangerous if swallowed," but these chemical, synthetic products can also harm your dog through contact on his skin and paws. In an earlier chapter, we mentioned applying essential oils to the pads of your dog's feet because the oils are readily absorbed into his body this way. Potentially harmful chemicals are also readily absorbed through the pads of your dog's feet and through his skin. The ingredients in chemical, synthetic yard products are cumulative in your dog's body. That means that these chemicals will always stay in her body and will eventually cause a decline in health unless you take steps to detoxify her with natural products, and remove the chemicals from her environment to prevent repeated exposure. Symptoms of stress, anxiety, and even mental decline in your dog can be the direct result of his being in contact with yard chemicals or floor cleaning chemicals. Seizures are another allergic reaction that dogs can have when in contact with pesticides or chemical fertilizers.

Remember that since dogs are biological, organic beings, what affects them can and will affect us also.

Many of you may think your yard will fall apart if you don't use these chemicals, or that natural alternatives are too expensive. In reality, by switching to natural, organic products, you can save a bundle in veterinarian and doctor bills for your dog and yourself in the long run, not to mention saving the environment. When you switch to all-natural yard care, it will take a while for your yard to detoxify and "come clean," but eventually you will bring back the natural eco-balance where all life can thrive—including your dog.

Paint

Yes, it's true that there are a lot of safer paints on the market today, but we would venture to say that drinking them will never be safe. Dogs use their mouths like hands, to sample and feel as well as to taste things, so it's always best to keep open paint cans away from your dog. If ingested, paint can also cause allergy symptoms resembling hay fever or skin disorders.

The first step you can take is to always be sure that the paint you choose is the least toxic, most child-safe kind you can find. Make sure your home is well ventilated when painting, because if you think the fumes bother you, think about how your dog feels. Because a dog's sense of smell is far greater than that of a human, inhaling these toxic fumes can be extremely detrimental to her health. You may notice your dog acting anxious, stressed, or overexcited or suddenly start having skin rashes and hair loss after coming into contact with paints. These toxins most commonly enter our dogs (and us) through the skin and by inhalation. They accumulate in the body, and over time will wear down the immune system, making it more susceptible to disease.

 The Garage Can Be a Very Unsafe Place

We commonly keep lots of toxic chemicals in our garages, from paints to coolants to chemical fertilizers. Dogs are frequently brought in to veterinarian clinics with antifreeze or coolant poisoning, and many, if not most, do not survive. Dogs like the taste of coolant and oil and will often do their best to ingest these substances if they are left lying around.

Keep your dog out of your garage, or keep these harmful chemicals locked up where your dog can't reach them. If you change your oil or coolant, please dispose of it responsibly at a toxic-waste dump, and do not leave it in a place your dog has access to. Once a dog has ingested one of these products, he will decline rapidly, going into shock and falling unconsciousness, and he may ultimately die unless he gets immediate care by your veterinarian. If you suspect your dog has ingested any of these products, get him to your veterinarian immediately. Keep him warm and use homeopathic treatments on the way to your veterinarian, and be sure to bring the container of the suspected product with you.

Indoor Chemicals

A study done in the United States in 1989 discovered that 50 percent of all illness is due to poor air quality in the home. This is due in large part to the fact that we like the convenience of using the popular "quick" household cleaners. We've traded wholesome, natural cleaners that might take more time to use for extremely toxic substances all in the name of convenience and ease. Another contributing factor is that our homes have become much "tighter" through the use of extra-thick insulation and thermal windows and doors, in an effort to keep us warm while lowering heating costs. With a tighter home, you will have much less air flow, resulting in more humidity and a buildup of toxicity from all the chemicals used in homes today, leaving the air in your home very polluted.

We use so many chemicals in our homes that most of us aren't even aware that we are helping a toxic environment thrive within our own homes. Over the last thirty years, we've introduced more and more toxins in the form of cleaners and personal products. Some of the worst carcinogens are found in hair spray, air freshener, window cleaner, nail polish remover, laundry soap, furniture polish, floor care products, liquid dish soap, certain brands of toothpaste, hair coloring, bleach, and household disinfectant. These substances are harming not only us, but our pets as well.

Most dogs lie on floors that have been cleaned with highly toxic floor cleaners, carpets that have been sprinkled with toxic powders to remove odors, and bedding that has been washed in toxic chemical laundry soaps. While we may wear gloves to clean our homes, the chemicals from these products linger in the air we breathe.

These toxins accumulate in our dogs' bodies (and ours), eventually causing a state of disease. All of these chemical products will affect our dogs faster than us because they are usually closer to the source (on the floor) and have a heightened sense of smell. Diseases and illness can range and vary from allergies, respiratory problems, autoimmune disorders, liver and kidney disorders, and even cancer.

We may already be treating some of these symptoms thinking that we are allergic to something else, such as plants, flowers, or weeds. Our immune systems and those of our dogs are trying to repel these toxins, masking them as the symptoms of allergies, respiratory infections, nausea, and so on.

Mold

Another contributor to poor air quality in our homes is mold. Mold is also on the rise because of the way we've made our homes "tighter." While some mold is in every home, toxic black mold is the dangerous form that can kill.

Dogs will get symptoms of sinus and respiratory problems that are often treated with allergy medicines or even antibiotics. However, mold is not histamine-driven, so antihistamines won't work, and according to Dr. George Graham of Mold Lab International (www.themoldlab.com), mold is also resistant to antibiotics. So, once again, the overmedication of dogs becomes a problem. It is also important to note that bleach does nothing more than turn mold white, so it does nothing to eliminate a mold problem. In fact, by attempting to rectify the situation with bleach, you are adding more noxious, dangerous chemical fumes to the air in your home.

Natural Alternatives to Environmental Toxins

There is a saying in homeopathy that within every problem is the solution, or within every disease lies the cure. The same holds true for our chemical-laden environment. Before all these chemicals were used, nature provided us with our cleaning, personal hygiene, and vegetation protection sources. We turned away from those sources for the sake of convenience, but fortunately, they still exist.

Detoxification

The only way to remove these toxins and petrochemicals from your dog's body is through a detoxifying cleanse. This should be done under the supervision of your holistic veterinarian. When a dog is detoxifying, she can go through what is called a healing crisis, and needs to be monitored. While the cleanse is good and necessary, it isn't usually a fun ordeal for you or your dog. The best thing you can do is avoid the need for it by using natural products in and around your home.

Replacing Outdoor Chemicals

Some of the methods for pest control and prevention mentioned in chapter eight are effective also for controlling pests in your yard. The same things that repel fleas, ticks, and mosquitoes will also repel other bugs.

German Shorthaired Pointers

Diatomaceous earth is very effective and inexpensive and is harmless to us, our pets, and the environment. The only thing it harms is the bugs we want to get rid of. It is not a chemical; it acts like cutting glass against the exoskeleton of parasites and bugs. Bugs will instinctively steer clear of your yard when you use this product. You can also spray your yard with an essential oil mixture. Some great bug repellents include peppermint, spearmint, cedarwood, thyme, lavender, lemongrass, and pine.

Praying mantis

Lady bug

Nature has also provided some wonderful natural predators to take out destructive parasites and pests. Ladybugs, lacewings, and praying mantises are all predatory bugs that like to feed on things such as aphids and other nasty pests. For every single parasite, nature has provided a counterattack. For slugs and snails, turtles are the perfect predator, and turtles can eat a ton of those creatures. For lawn grubs, natural parasites called beneficial nematodes or a substance called milky spore will work great. Both are natural and will not hurt beneficial insects such as ladybugs and bees. By encouraging populations of these natural predators (i.e., not spraying your yard with chemicals to eradicate every living thing), you'll create an eco-friendly yard where birds and other wildlife will thrive.

In addition, there are many commercial organic fertilizers you can purchase either locally or by mail order (see Resources, page 168). Or you can make your own fertilizer using a composter. By building a healthy lawn with nature's ingredients, you'll create an ecosystem that is in balance and is naturally effective at fighting off predators and disease—functioning just like your immune system. When you create this environment for your dog (and your children), you won't have to worry about them lying in the grass or eating it. (Grass is another natural nutrient your dog can and will enjoy for his good health.)

Replacing Indoor Chemicals

You might not replace all your indoor chemicals overnight, but the best place to begin is to eliminate your chemical cleaning and personal care products and replace them with natural, organic products. They might be more expensive in some instances, but the long-term savings come with reduced veterinarian and medical costs for you and your pets. A very good and very inexpensive product you can clean your floors and windows with is white vinegar and warm water. White vinegar can also double as an inexpensive ear-cleaning solution for your dog's ears (See recipe in chapter one).

Do some research into natural, wholesome products to clean your home and do laundry with, and for your and your dog's personal grooming. Unfortunately, because natural is a popular term these days and is largely unregulated on labels, many products really aren't natural and include many of the same harmful chemicals that regular products do. Due diligence in your research is imperative. There are far too many companies and products to list in one chapter, but we do provide some suggestions in the Resource section of this book.

Other indoor pollutants that can be easily replaced are air fresheners and carpet powders. If, after reading chapters eight and nine, you are already diffusing essential oils in your home, great. If not, this is a wonderful reason to do it. In fact, many of the oils can be used mixed with water or baking soda to do household cleaning.

For example, take a small box of baking soda, poke a hole down into the baking soda inside the box (as if you were going to plant a seed in it), and add twenty to thirty drops of lemon essential oil. Let it absorb into the baking soda, and then mix it up and use it as a scouring cleaner in place of your regular chlorine-type scouring cleanser. In place of a standard aerosol air freshener, mix a few drops of your favorite essential oil with purified water in an amber or blue glass spray bottle (to keep the integrity of the oils intact, as light can destroy them), and use that as your air freshener. The essential oils can clean the air in your home even better than an air filter can, and they will also detoxify you and your dog.

To remove mold spores from the air in your home and prevent mold growth naturally, Dr. Graham of Mold Lab International (www.themoldlab.com) offers a solution of grapefruit seed extract or tea tree (melaleuca) oil, which can be purchased on the website.

Moving Forward

Labrador Retriever

As we embarked upon this journey into natural dog health and disease prevention, our goal was to help you discover some different ways to help your dog live a longer, fuller life. By addressing controversial subjects such as vaccinating and feeding methods, we hope we've given you a new perspective from which to view them, and the knowledge to make the best decisions for you and your dog. Most importantly, we've shown you what health is and how to care for your dog naturally—the way that is most beneficial for him, you, and the environment. Our joy has been sharing what whole health means for your happy dog.

10 Natural Health Essentials for a Happy, Healthy Dog

1. Take your dog for regular yearly checkups.

2. Make sure your dog is spayed or neutered.

3. Feed your dog a natural, wholesome diet that includes supplements.

4. Don't overvaccinate—get blood titers first to see if vaccinations are necessary.

5. Exercise your dog to keep him fit, trim, and happy.

6. Keep a natural emergency kit on hand.

7. Use natural preventions and remedies instead of, or to complement, traditional medicines.

8. Groom your dog regularly.

9. Remove as many chemical factors as possible from your home and yard and replace them with natural, organic products.

10. Know your dog is unique and care for her according to her own uniqueness.

Appendix

Appendix A: Breeds

Sporting Dogs

Golden Retriever, Labrador Retriever, Cocker Spaniel, Springer Spaniel, Irish Setter, Vizla

Typically, these breeds are very high-energy and need a lot of exercise. They love to please humans, so they are also easier to train than other breeds. Most sporting dogs need frequent grooming, with the possible exception of the Vizla or Labrador (due to their shorter coats).

Size range: medium (as in the Springer Spaniel) to large (as in the Labrador or Golden Retriever).

Hounds

Afghan Hound, Basset Hound, Beagle, Bloodhound, Dachshund, Greyhound, Borzoi, Irish Wolfhound, Rhodesian Ridgeback, Whippet

Hounds aren't as energetic as the sporting breeds, but they do require some daily exercise. This group can be very independent thinking, which can make them harder to train for obedience. Patience with kind but firm persistence is needed. Most dogs in this group are fairly easy to groom with the exception of the Afghan Hound, which has a long, fine, silky coat.

Size range: medium (as in the Basset Hound) to giant (as in the Irish Wolfhound or Borzoi).

Working Dogs

Alaskan Malamute, Belgian Tervuren, Bernese Mountain Dog, Boxer, Bouvier des Flandres, Bullmastiff, German Shepherd, Great Dane, Mastiff, Newfoundland, Rottweiler, Siberian Husky, Akita, Collie, Great Pyrenees, Old English Sheepdog, Samoyed, Welsh Corgi, St. Bernard

This is a tough and tenacious group, often with great strength. They were primarily bred for heavy manual labor and as guardians for humans and livestock. Because of this, they are independent thinkers, and you will need due diligence in training and a firm, but loving hand in raising them. The working dogs do need regular exercise, and some of the breeds need lots of grooming.

Size range: medium (as in the Welsh Corgi) to giant (as in the Mastiff).

Terriers

Airedale Terrier, American Staffordshire, Bedlington Terrier, Bull Terrier, Cairn Terrier, Fox Terrier, Rat Terrier, Jack Russell Terrier, Scottish Terrier, West Highland White Terrier

Terriers have long been known as stubborn, tenacious, and energetic. Exercise is a must, as many breeds in this group were designed for endurance and strength. Training is also imperative with this group, and should not be taken lightly. Otherwise, they will rule your home. Grooming can be simple, as with a Jack Russell, or require lots of regular visits to a groomer, as with a Bedlington.

Size range: small such (as in the Fox Terrier) to large (as in the Airedale).

Toys

Miniature Pinchser, Chihuahua, Maltese, Toy Poodle, Pug, Shih Tzu, Yorkshire Terrier, Pomeranian, Pekingese

Most of the toy dogs were designed to be lap dogs for royalty, and they are still popular for this reason today. Training this group can be difficult, simply because they are so small that people think they can't or shouldn't be disciplined. Some toy dogs require very little grooming, such as the Chihuahua, while others need a lot of grooming, such the Yorkshire.

Size range: tiny (as in the Miniature Pinscher) to small (as in the Shih Tzu).

Non-Sporting Dogs

Boston Terrier, Chow Chow, Lhasa Apso, Dalmatian, Poodle

Many dogs in this group could fit into one or more of the other groups. For instance, Poodles were used for hunting, and Chow Chows were used as guardians. However, they are most often thought of as companion dogs. This group needs regular exercise and attention. Grooming requirements vary in this group, with the Boston Terrier needing little brushing, and the Chow Chow needing a lot.

Size range: small such (as in the Boston Terrier) to large (as in the Standard Poodle).

Herding Dogs

Australian Cattle Dog, Border Collie, Australian Shepherd

This group was bred to herd—period. Their main desire is to herd something, anyone, anything, and they focus intently on it. If you are looking for a low maintenance, low-energy dog, you won't find one in this group! They are not the independent thinking types, but live to please and be with their humans. They also require regular grooming, particularly when working a lot.

Size range: medium (as in the Border Collie) to large (as in the Australian Shepherd).

Appendix B: Breed Specific Diseases

(Not all breeds or diseases are listed.)

Breed	Disease
Afghan Hound	Cataracts, elbow joint malformation, hypothyroidism, susceptibility to hepatitis, third eyelid eversion
Airedale Terrier	Cancer (lymph system and pancreas), skin disorders, colon diseases
Akita	Deafness, elbow and hip dysplasia, hypo- and hyperthyroidism, skin disorders
Alaskan Malamute	Anemia, dwarfism, hip dysplasia, eye disorders
Australian Cattle Dog	Deafness, eczema
Australian Shepherd	Diabetes mellitus, Legg-Perthes disease
Basset Hound	Deformed spine resulting in paralysis, immunodeficiency, seizures, dermatitis, bloat, blood disorders, glaucoma
Beagle	Dermatitis, bladder cancer, cataracts, cleft palate, deafness, epilepsy, glaucoma
Bernese Mountain Dog	Cleft palate, elbow and hip dysplasia, umbilical hernias
Bloodhound	Bloat, external ear infections, hematoma (blood clot on ear flap), moist dermatitis (hot spots), bone-growth problems
Border Collie	Eye disorders (corneal dystrophy, blindness), deafness
Boston Terrier	Cleft palate, Cushing's syndrome, deafness, glaucoma, skin disorders, tumors
Boxer	Tumors, deafness, skin disorders, bloat, hypothyroidism, melanoma
Brittany	Epilepsy, hip dysplasia
Bulldog	Lymphoma (cancer), elbow and hip dysplasia, eye and bone disorders, spina bifida
Bull Mastiff	Bloat, elbow and hip dysplasia, glaucoma, eye disorders
Cavalier King Charles Spaniel	Cataracts, diabetes
Chihuahua	Cleft palate, eye disorders, fatty liver syndrome, hypoglycemia
Chinese Shar-Pei	Elbow and hip dysplasia, inflammatory bowel syndrome (IBS), skin staph infections, joint and bone disorders, cherry eyes (third eyelid problems)

Breed	Disease
Chow Chow	Bloat, hormone abnormalities, cataracts, cleft palate, elbow and hip dysplasia, hypothyroidism
Cocker Spaniel	Allergies, chronic hepatitis, deafness, elbow, hip and kidney dysplasia, glaucoma, seborrhea
Collie	Bladder cancer, deafness, dwarfism, epilepsy, eye disorders
Dachshund	Cleft palate, deafness, dermatitis, diabetes, hypothyroidism
Dalmatian	Dermatitis, deafness, glaucoma
Doberman Pinscher	Chronic hepatitis, deafness, elbow dysplasia, immune disorders, narcolepsy, vitiligo
English Springer Spaniel	Retinal atrophy, diabetes, epilepsy, glaucoma, hip dysplasia
Fox Terrier	Cataracts, colonic disease, deafness, glaucoma, goiter
French Bulldog	Cleft palate, hemophilia
German Shepherd	Behavior abnormalities, bowel disorders, deafness, elbow and hip dysplasia, dermatitis, epilepsy, hypothyroidism, seborrhea, progressive posterior paralysis (lower half of body)
German Shorthaired Pointer	Corneal dystrophy, cancer (fibrosarcoma, melanoma)
Golden Retriever	Acute moist dermatitis (hot spots), cataracts, elbow and hip dysplasia, allergies, muscular dystrophy
Great Dane	Lick dermatitis, deafness, elbow and hip dysplasia, metabolic bone disease, hypothyroidism, bone cancer, heart disease
Great Pyrenees	Cataracts, deafness, defective heart, hip dysplasia, dwarfism
Greyhound	Bloat, retinal dystrophy
Irish Setter	Lick dermatitis, cataracts and other eye disorders, allergies, hip dysplasia, seborrhea
Irish Wolfhound	Cataracts, heart disease, elbow and hip dysplasia, bone cancer
Jack Russell Terrier	Skin disorders, deafness
Keeshond	Epilepsy, hypothyroidism, heart disease
Labrador Retriever	Atherosclerosis, lick dermatitis, cataracts, chronic hepatitis, eye disorders, diabetes, dwarfism, epilepsy, hip dysplasia, hypoglycemia, hypothyroidism, melanoma, seborrhea
Lhasa Apso	Corneal ulcers, hip dysplasia, allergies, kidney disorders

Breed	Disease
Maltese	Blindness, deafness, hypoglycemia
Mastiff	Bloat, elbow dysplasia
Miniature Pinscher	Prone to shoulder dislocation, retinal atrophy (eye disorder), skin disease (lack of pigmentation)
Newfoundland	Bloat, cardiomyopathy (heart spasms), elbow and hip dysplasia, moist dermatitis (hot spots)
Old English Sheepdog	Bloat, cataracts, hip dysplasia, Wobbler's syndrome
Pekinese	Numerous eye disorders, palate disorders
Pointer	Colonic disease, deafness, epilepsy, hip dysplasia, eye disorders
Pomeranian	Shoulder problems, dwarfism, elephant skin, eye disorders
Poodle	Behavioral problems, eye and ear disorders, Cushing's syndrome, epilepsy, skin disorders, glaucoma, heart disease; standard size also prone to hip dysplasia
Pug	Numerous eye and breathing disorders
Rottweiler	Diabetes, elbow and hip dysplasia, congenital deafness
St. Bernard	Cardiomyopathy, deafness, diabetes, elbow and hip dysplasia, gastric torsion (bloat), osteosarcoma (bone cancer)
Samoyed	Diabetes, dwarfism, dermatitis, glaucoma, hip dysplasia, sebaceous cysts
Schnauzer	Allergies, pancreatitis
Shih Tzu	Cleft palate, allergies, ulcers of the cornea, and other eye disorders
Siberian Husky	Eye disorders, epilepsy, hip dysplasia
Staffordshire Bull Terrier	Cataracts, cleft palate
Vizsla	Hemophilia, hip dysplasia
Weimaraner	Bloat, dwarfism, fibrosarcoma, hip dysplasia, undershot jaw
Welsh Corgi	Eye disorders, glaucoma
West Highland White Terrier	Cataracts, chronic hepatitis, deafness, fatty liver syndrome, hip dysplasia, seborrhea
Whippet	Demodetic mange
Yorkshire Terrier	Enlarged head, fatty liver syndrome, skin disorders

Appendix C: Treatments and Supplements for Common Diseases

Disease/Ailment	Remedy/Supplement	Dosage
Anemia (when due to hemmorage)	Ferrum phosphoricum	6C potency 3 times a day
	Arnica and Aconitum (esp. from trauma or shock), Phosphorous, Hammamelis, or Lachesis	30C every 5 to 10 minutes; if one remedy doesn't work after three doses, move to the next remedy
Arthritis	Vitamin C (supplement)	5–15 mg/lb, two to three times a day
	CoEnzQ10 (supplement)	1–2 mg/lb, two to three times a day
	Glucosamine sulfate, usually combined with Chondroitin sulfate (supplement)	5–10 mg/lb twice a day
	Tumeric (spice, esp. for inflammation) (supplement)	a pinch added to regular food
	Bromelain (for pain relief) (supplement)	5–10 mg/lb, two to three times a day
	Rhus toxicodendron, Calcarea, Fluorica, Hecla lava, Arnica, Belladonna, Bryonia	6X or 6C, two times a day for chronic pain; 30C as needed for acute pain. If remedy doesn't show results after three doses, another remedy should be given.
Bladder Infection	Cranberry Comfort (supplement)	once a day, depending on weight of dog
	Kali muriaticum	6X or 6C twice a day for ten days
Breast Tumors	*First, see a vet.* Transfer Factor Plus	follow manufacturer's instructions; see Resources
Distemper	*First, see a vet.* Hypericum	6C twice a day for ten to thirty days, then reevaluate.
Parvo	*First, see a vet.* Phosphorous, Arsenicum album, Veratrum album	30C, three times a day; if one remedy doesn't work after three doses, move to the next remedy
Epilepsy	*First, see a vet.* Belladonna	30C; mix pellets w/ half glass of water and apply ½ dropper to lips or any hairless part of dog's body at first sign of seizure
Eye Problems	Optique 1 (eye drops)	two drops three to four times a day in affected eye(s)
	Euphrasia	30C given orally once or twice a day for 3–5 days
	Acountium	30C administered every fifteen minutes during the first hour following trauma (on the way to the vet)
	Vitamin C (supplement)	5–10 mg/lb, 2–3 times a day
	Vitamin E (supplement)	5–10 mg/lb, once a day
Foreign Body (due to puncture wound or swallowing of foreign object)	Silicea (see a veterinarian)	30C, 2–3 times a day for one to three days

Disease/Ailment	Remedy/Supplement	Dosage
Hair Loss	Thuja	30C once a day for three days. Reevaluate after three to four weeks.
Heart	*First, see a vet.* Hawthorne tincture	10 drops in dog's water daily
Hip and Elbow Dysplasia	Rhus toxicodendron, Calcarea carbonica; may also use supplements listed for arthritis, above	3 pellets (30C) weekly; if dog shows no improvement after three weeks, try the other remedy
Jaundice	Milk thistle tincture (to support liver) (supplement)	10 drops in dog's water daily
	Cheledonium	6X or 6C, once or twice daily administer for three days then reevaluate.
	Hydrastis, Lycopodium (to support liver)	30C one dose and reevaluate in three to four weeks.
Kidney Failure	Lacerated Ringers Solution	Based on vet's recommendations; injected daily
	Burberis vulgaris (early or middle-stage disease)	6C or 12C, once or twice daily; in dry pellet form or dissolved in bottled, distilled, or filtered water
	Apis mellifica (end stage disease) tea made from any combination of alfalfa, nettles, dandelion (supplement)	30C once a day for three days in addition to above ½ dropper for every 10 pounds, 2–3 times a day
Liver Problems	See Jaundice, above	
Pancreatitis	*First, see a vet.* Iris versicolor	6X or 6C twice a day
Paralysis	*First, see a vet.* Hypericum (for nerve damage)	30C twice a day for 3–5 days; if you see improvement. If no improvement, see homeopathic consultant.
Skin	*First, see a vet.* Apis mellifica (symptoms of bee sting: red, swollen, hives, itchy); Firnuca rufa (itchy, red all over); Rhus toxicodendron (poison ivy/oak); Ledum palustre (puncture wounds, insect bites); Uritica urens (intense itching)	administer one remedy at a time, 30C once a day for 3–5 days; if little to no improvement, move on to another remedy
	Hypercal lotion (external lesions)	one part lotion to ten parts distilled water, applied with clean gauze pad 2–3 times a day topically
Hot Spots	Apis mellifica (red, swollen); Belladonna (sudden, violent itching, irritable, fever); Graphites (yellow discharge, lesions); Hepar sulphur (oozing yellow discharge, irritable and sensitive to touch); Mercurious vivus or solubilis (ulcers, irritable, resists examination)	apply topically once a day for three days
	Hypercal solution (see skin)	one part lotion to ten parts distilled water, applied with clean gauze pad 2–3 times a day

Disease/Ailment	Remedy/Supplement	Dosage
Ringworm	Bacillinum	200C once a week for four weeks
Regurgiation (food comes out whole, undigested)	Phosphorous	30C once a day for three days; if no improvement, see a vet
Stomach or Digestive Problems	Nux vomica (diarrhea from eating garbage); Arsenicum alba (chilly, restless); Aloe (nonpainful diarrhea, with gas); Lycopodium (diarrhea, gas); Mercurius vivus or solubilis (difficulty with bowel movements, stool contains blood or mucus); Podophyllum (watery, painless diarrhea with mucus); Sulphur (sudden diarrhea; red, inflamed anus)	30C when dog experiences symptoms; administer up to three times, and then try another remedy; see vet if condition persists after one day of treatment
	Slippery Elm, Aloe Juice (supplements)	¼ teaspoon for small dogs, ½ teaspoon for medium-sized dogs, 1 teaspoon for large dogs, 1½ teaspoons for giant breeds; administer once or twice a day
Thyroid Problems	Kelp, Iodine (supplements that provide trace elements)	one tablet per ten pounds daily
	Thyrophin PMG (supplement)	follow the low end of the dose according to manufacturer's instructions
Upper Respiratory Infections	*First, see a vet. Then, if problem is simple (i.e. not bronchitis or pneumonia) try:* Allium cepa (hay fever-like symptoms, worse in cold weather); Arsenicum album (chilly, thirsty, restless); Calcarea sulphurica (yellow discharge from nose); Kali bichromicum (heavy, crusty discharge and difficulty breathing through nose); Silicea (when all else fails!)	30C once a day for 3–5 days; if one remedy doesn't work, try another; if if condition worsens, revisit your vet
Vomiting	Ipecacuanha	30C when vomiting occurs; withhold food and drink for twelve to twenty hours. If vomiting does not cease after three doses, see a veterinarian.
Warts	Thuja occidentalis (general), Staphysagria (esp. for warts in the mouth, gums, cheeks, anus)	30C once a week for four weeks

Resources

Associations

The American Holistic Veterinary Medical Association
Dr. Carvel G. Tiekert,
Executive Director
2218 Old Emmorton Road
Bel Air, MD 21015 USA
Phone: 410.569.0795
Fax: 410.569.2346
Email: office@ahvma.org
www.ahvma.org

Academy of Veterinary Homeopathy
PO Box 9280
Wilmington, DE 19809 USA
Phone and fax: 866.652.1590 (US and Canada)
www.theavh.org

American Academy of Veterinary Acupuncture
100 Roscommon Drive, Suite 320
Middletown, CT 06457 USA
Phone: 860.635.6300
Fax: 860.635.6400
Email: office@aava.org
www.aava.org

American Veterinary Chiropractic Association
442154 E 140 Rd.
Bluejacket, OK 74333 USA
Phone: 918.784.2231
Fax: 918.784.2675
www.animalchiropractic.org

Magazines

Animal Wellness, PMB 168
8174 S. Holly St.
Centennial, CO 80122 USA

164 Hunter St. W
Peterborough, Ontario, Canada
K9H 2L2
Phone: 866-764-1212
www.animalwellnessmagazine.com

The Whole Dog Journal
Editorial Offices:
1175 Regent Street
Alameda, CA 94501 USA
E-mail: WholeDogJ@aol.com
www.whole-dog-journal.com

Rescue and Humane Organizations

www.noahswish.org
www.americanhumane.org
www.petfinders.org
www.1-800-SAVE-A-PET.com
www.BestFriends.org

Homeopathic Pharmacies

Hahnemann Laboratories
San Rafael, CA USA
Contact: Michael Quinn
Phone: 888.427.6422
Fax: 415.451.6981
E-mail: michael@hahnemannlabs
.com
www.hahnemannlabs.com

Helios Homeopathic Pharmacy
97 Camden Road
Tunbridge Wells
Kent, England TN1 2QR UK
Phone: 44.01892.537.254
44.01892.536393 (24 hours)
Fax: 0044.01892.546.850
E-mail: pharmacy@helios.co.uk
www.helios.co.uk
They sell travelers kits of thirty-six remedies (DH36T) in 30C potencies, as well as many other kits.

Natural Health Supply
Santa Fe, NM USA
Phone: 505.474.9175
Fax: 505.473.0336

Holistic Veterinarians and Training Centers

You can find veterinarians throughout the United States and Canada who practice homeopathy by logging onto the Web site of the Academy of Veterinary Homeopathy (www.theAVH.org). They are listed by the states in which they practice, and the directory indicates how much of their practice is devoted to homeopathy versus conventional medicine.

Dr. Richard Pitcairn of the Animal Natural Health Center provides a referral list of graduates of his programs throughout the United States and Canada (www.drpitcairn.com/referrals/anhc_referrals.html). Dr. Pitcairn also offers training courses in and audiotapes on homeopathic treatment of animals for veterinarians (www.drpitcairn.com/index.html).

Homeopathic Training for Health Professionals
28 Beaumont Street
Oxford OX1 2NP UK
Phone: 44.1865.552706
www.hptg.org
Offers two different certificate programs—one for primary health professionals and one for veterinarians. Also provides a referral list of veterinarians in the United Kingdom, Australia, and parts of Europe.

Australian Holistic Veterinarians (primarily homeopathy)
Dr. Douglas Wilson, BVM&S, PhD, VetMFHom, MACVSc
The Holistic Veterinary Clinic
308 Glen Osmond Road
Fullarton 5063
South Australia
Phone: 61.8.8338.0005
Fax 61.8.8338.0007
E-mail: douglaswilson@
ozemail.com.au

The Bella Moss Foundation and Pets MRSA (UK)
Phone: 44.0786.0879.079
E-mail: info@thebellamoss
foundation.com
www.thebellamossfoundation.com
www.pets-mrsa.com

Dr. Richard Allport, DVM
Natural Medicine Centre
11 Southgate Road
Potters Bar
Herts EN6 5DR UK
Phone: 44.1707.662058
Fax: 44.1707.646948
E-mail: info@naturalmedicinecentre
.net
www.naturalmedicinecentre.net

Christopher Aust
Master Dog Trainer
12085 Rock Creek Road, #18
Auburn, CA 95602 USA
Phone: 530.889.8106
E-mail: chris@master-dog-training
.com
www.master-dog-training.com

Dr. Nancy Brandt, DVM
Phone consults on using therapeutic grade essential oils with pets.
Phone: 702.617.3285

Sources for Environmentally Friendly Home and Garden Products

Garden Harvest Supply
2952W 500S
Berne, IN 46711 USA
www.gardenharvestsupply.com
Natural lawn and yard products

Gardens Alive
5100 Schenley Place
Lawrenceburg, IN 47025 USA
Phone: 513.354.1483
www.gardensalive.com
Natural yard, garden, home, and pet-care products

Gaiam
www.gaiam.com
Natural products for the home and yard

Orvis
Manchester, VT USA
Phone: 866.531.6188
www.orvis.com
Premium pet care products

Flower Essences
Rescue Remedy
www.bachflower.com/rescue_remedy.htm. Rescue Remedy is made up of five flower essences: star of Bethlehem, clematis, cherry plum, impatiens, and rock rose. In addition, 27 percent alcohol is added as a preservative. Rescue Remedy is used for a variety of things from stress to trauma. It helps calm your dog and is especially effective for traveling.

Edible Oils
Wilderness Family Naturals
Box 538
Finland, MN 55603 USA
Email: info@wildnernissnaturalfamily
.com
www.wildernessnaturalfamily.com
Coconut oil, supplements, herbs

Diffusers & Aromatherapy Supplies
Abundant Health
1460 North Main St. #9
Spanish Fork, UT 84660 USA
Toll-Free Order: 1.800.718.3068
Email: orders@abundanthealth.us
www.abundanthealth.us

All-Natural Suppliers
Dinovite Inc.
2305 Lemon Northcutt Rd.
Dry Ridge, KY 41035 USA
Ed Lukacelic
Phone: 859.428.1000
Email: ed@dinovite.com
www.dinovite.com
Whole food supplement for dogs

The Natural Canine
163 Belden Falls Rd.
New Haven, VT 05472 USA
Phone: 802.388.2137
Email: questions@naturalcanine
.com
www.naturalcanine.com
Herbal supplements, remedies, flower esscences, homeopathy, etc.

Additional Resources
Dr. George Graham
The Mold Lab
7417 Kingston Pike, Suite 301A
Knoxville, TN 37919 USA
Phone: 865.558.9772
www.themoldlab.com
Mold removal

Aspenbloom
Albuquerque, NM 87109 USA
Phone : 505-217-1815
E-mail: info@aspenbloom.com
www.aspenbloom.com
Therapeutic-grade essential oils, natural dog grooming products, internal body cleanse, whole food supplements, enzymes, EFAS, diffusers, natural cleaning products

Bright Wings, Inc.
1858 Pleasantville Road #166
Briarcliff Manor, NY 10510-1025
USA
Phone: 888-833-1725
www.floweressencesforanimals.com
Flower essences

Only Natural Pet
Herbal remedies for dogs, enzymes, probiotics
Phone: 888-937-6677
www.onlynaturalpet.com

Animal Talk Naturally
www.animaltalknaturally.com
Online talk show

Food Resources
www.naturesvariety.com
www.honestkitchen.com
www.canz.com
www.sojos.com
www.amorepetfoods.com

REFERENCES AND SUGGESTED READING

On Vaccination

O' Driscoll, Catherine. *What Vets Don't Tell You About Vaccines*. London, England: Abbeywood Publishing, 1993.

O' Driscoll, Catherine. *Who Killed the Darling Buds of May?* London, England: Abbeywood Publishing, 1997.

    O' Driscoll has written several books on the dangers of vaccinations and overvaccinating. She uses her experiences with her own beloved Golden Retrievers to fuel the passion she has for seeing new vaccine protocols implemented.

Shultz, Ronald R. (1998). *Current & Future Canine and Feline Vaccination Programs*. Vet Med3: No. 3, 233-254.

www.minimum.com/b.asp?a=veterinary-vaccination-hamilton

www.canine-health-concern.org.uk/

www.home.earthlink.net/~petsfriend/vaccinations.html www.labbies.com/immun.htm

www.petitiononline.com/petvax23/ www.dogsadversereactions.com/classaction.html www.thepetcenter.com/exa/vac.html

On Feeding

Brown, Steve; Taylor, Beth. *See Spot Live Longer: How to Help Your Dog Live a Longer and Healthier Life*. Eugene, OR: Creekobear Press, 2004.

Lewis, Lon D.; Morris, Mark L., Jr.; Hand, Michael S. *Small Animal Nutrition III*. Topeka, KS: Mark Morris Associates, 1990.

Martin, Ann. *Foods Pets Die For*. Troutdale, OR: NewSage Press, 2002

Roberts, Donna Twichell. *The Good Food Cookbook for Dogs*. Gloucester, MA: Quarry Books, 2004.

On Overall Holistic Care

Callahan, Jean. *Your Older Dog*. East Sussex, UK: Apple Press, 2001.

Garvey, Michael S., DVM, et al. *The Veterinarian's Guide to Your Dog's Symptoms*. New York: Villard, 1999.

Goldstein, Martin. *The Nature of Animal Healing*. New York: Random House, 2000.

O'Driscoll, Catherine. *What Vets Don't Tell You About Vaccines*. London, UK: Abbeywood Publishing, 1993.

Pitcairn, Richard H. *Natural Health for Dogs and Cats*. New York: Rodale Press, 2005

Prevention Magazine. *The Doctors Book of Home Remedies for Dogs and Cats*. New York: Rodale, 2002.

Shanahan, Niki Behrikis. *There Is Eternal Life for Animals*. Tyngsborough, MA: Pete Publishing, 2005

Schoen, Allen M. et al (eds.). *Veterinary Acupuncture: Ancient Art to Modern Medicine*. New York: C.V. Mosby, 1994.

Polhard, Wendy; Brown, Kerry L. *Holistic Guide for a Healthy Dog*. New York: Wiley, 2000.

On First Aid, Homeopathic Care, and Healing

Allport, Richard. *Heal Your Dog the Natural Way*. New York: Howell Book House, 1997.

Brown, Kathleen. *10 Herbs for Happy, Healthy Dogs*. North Adams, MA: Storey Books, 2000.

Essential Science Publishing Staff. *Essential Oils Desk Reference*. Orem, UT: Essential Science Publishing, 2004.

Fox, Michael W. *Healing Touch for Dogs: The Proven Massage Program for Dogs*. New York: Newmarket Press, 2004.

Graham, Helen; Vlamis, Gregory. *Bach Flower Remedies for Animals*. Forres, Scotland: Findhorn Press, 1999.

Hamilton, Don. *Homeopathic Care for Cats and Dogs: Small Doses for Small Animals*. Berkeley, CA: North Atlantic Books, 1999.

Hershoff, Asa. *Homeopathy for Musculoskeletal Healing*. Berkeley, CA: North Atlantic Books, 1996.

Kamen, Daniel R. *The Well Adjusted Dog: Canine Chiropractic Methods You Can Do*. Cambridge, MA: Brookline Books, 1997.

Macleod, George. *Cats: Homeopathic Remedies*. Saffron Walden, UK: C. W. Daniel, 1991.

Schnaubelt, Kurt. *Medical Aromatherapy: Healing with Essential Oils*. Berkeley, CA: Frog, Ltd., 1999.

Stein, Diane. *Natural Healing for Dogs & Cats*. Freedom, CA: Crossing Press, 1993.

Straw, Deborah. *Why Is Cancer Killing Our Pets?: How You Can Protect and Treat Your Companion Animal*. Rochester, VT: Healing Arts Press, 2000.

Worwood, Valerie Ann. *The Complete Book of Essential Oils and Aromatherapy*. Novato, CA: New World Library, 1991.

Zucker, Martin. *Veterinarians' Guide to Natural Remedies for Dogs: Safe and Effective Alternative Treatments and Healing Techniques from the Nation's Top Holistic Veterinarians*. New York: Three Rivers Press, 2000.